DON'T LET THE DEVIL STEAL YOUR SONG!

A MEMOIR OF RECOVERY FROM PARENTAL DIVORCE

CAROLYN COGSWELL

With 20 Essentials for Finding Your Sweet Spot

WESTBOW
PRESS®
A DIVISION OF THOMAS NELSON
& ZONDERVAN

Copyright © 2017 Carolyn Cogswell.

Also by the author
Weekly Insights for the Workplace: A Devotional for Christian Professionals
By Agnes Amos Coleman, Carolyn Cogswell

All rights reserved. No part of this book may be used or reproduced by any means, graphic, electronic, or mechanical, including photocopying, recording, taping or by any information storage retrieval system without the written permission of the author except in the case of brief quotations embodied in critical articles and reviews.

Scripture quotes marked (NKJV) are taken from the New King James Version®. Copyright © 1982 by Thomas Nelson. Used by permission. All rights reserved.
Scripture quotations marked (NIV) are taken from the Holy Bible, New International Version®, NIV®. Copyright © 1973, 1978, 1984, 2011 by Biblica, Inc.™ Used by permission of Zondervan. All rights reserved worldwide.
Scripture quotations taken from the New American Standard Bible® (NASB), Copyright © 1960, 1962, 1963, 1968, 1971, 1972, 1973, 1975, 1977, 1995 by The Lockman Foundation
Used by permission. www.Lockman.org
Scripture quotes marked (KJV) are taken from the King James Version of the Bible.

WestBow Press books may be ordered through booksellers or by contacting:

WestBow Press
A Division of Thomas Nelson & Zondervan
1663 Liberty Drive
Bloomington, IN 47403
www.westbowpress.com
1 (866) 928-1240

Because of the dynamic nature of the Internet, any web addresses or links contained in this book may have changed since publication and may no longer be valid. The views expressed in this work are solely those of the author and do not necessarily reflect the views of the publisher, and the publisher hereby disclaims any responsibility for them.

Any people depicted in stock imagery provided by Thinkstock are models, and such images are being used for illustrative purposes only.
Certain stock imagery © Thinkstock.

ISBN: 978-1-5127-8464-0 (sc)
ISBN: 978-1-5127-8466-4 (hc)
ISBN: 978-1-5127-8465-7 (e)

Library of Congress Control Number: 2017906507

Print information available on the last page.

WestBow Press rev. date: 10/03/2017

Essential – *n.*: 1. Something that is fundamental.
2. Something that is necessary or indispensable
(*The American Heritage Dictionary*, 1985).

Carolyn Cogswell takes an honest look at the long term effects of divorce on the children, often destroying their lives. The story is told by someone who lived through it painfully, and finally found peace, love and forgiveness in Jesus Christ. This book is a must read for professionals who analyze realities of divorce, and a must read for children of divorce still struggling with self-blame and looking for inner healing.

The thief does not come except to steal, and to kill, and to destroy. I have come that they may have life, and that they may have it more abundantly (John 10:10).

Contents

To David Cogswell ix
Don't Let the Devil Steal Your Song x
Preface xi
Acknowledgments xv
Introduction xvii

Chapter 1   Daddy's Little Girl – Gratitude 1
Chapter 2   Never Made It to Pretty Prairie – Good Grief 5
Chapter 3   Losing Daddy – Forgiveness 18
Chapter 4   His 'Real' Daughter – Identity 32
Chapter 5   Round Pegs in Square Holes – Purpose 41
Chapter 6   Gary Patched My Heart – Friends 53
Chapter 7   Relationships, False Havens of Rest – Healing 56
Chapter 8   Monday Blues – Courage 60
Chapter 9   Good Girl Gone Bad Gets Right – Purity 68
Chapter 10 Going to Grandma's – Wisdom 70
Chapter 11 Conquering Demons – Serenity 83
Chapter 12 The Gift of Getting Along – Kindness 88
Chapter 13 Hitting Bottom – Protection 92
Chapter 14 A Place You Don't Want to Go – Humility 96
Chapter 15 A Different Kind of High – Salvation 100

Chapter 16	Loves That Don't Love Back – Love God	102
Chapter 17	Seeing Jesus – Transformation	111
Chapter 18	Louisiana Lessons – Discernment	117
Chapter 19	Moving On – Hope	127
Chapter 20	Still My Hero – Patience	134

Appendix	141
The Recordings (1953-1958)	143
Dad's Eulogy	147
Devotion: The Resurrection and the Life	149
Who is Jesus?	151
Salvation Prayer	153
Knowing God is the Ultimate Privilege	155
'He Shines All Over': From Pretty Prairie to Omaha Beach	157
Final Words	171
Cogswell Family – Some Important Dates	173
Bibliography	179

To David Cogswell:

Every day we see ways our parents' divorce has affected our view of ourselves, our relationships, and the way we conduct our lives. Everyone may struggle with insecurities for different reasons, but we can pinpoint the beginning of ours.

Two major events remain before me: The first *major event* of my life is still our parents' divorce. The second *major event* of my life was the recognition of Jesus Christ as Lord of Creation and Lord of my life.

I hope the story will speak for itself; how Jesus acted in my behalf before my conversion, how he was always waiting for me to invite him into my life, how he heals my life now, how he is always with me, how he makes me know that he is the Lord, and why it makes a difference to have a relationship with him.

I am like the Samaritan woman in the fourth chapter of John who encountered Jesus at the well. As soon as she began to believe he was the Christ, she immediately went to tell everyone she knew to, "Come see a man who told me all things that I ever did …" (John 4:29).

I am deeply grateful for your presence in my life. You encouraged me to "put spiritual things first," to play music, and to write. You have always been willing to talk. You have been a source of inspiration, emotional support and intellectual stimulation.

This book is part family history, part testimony and part recovery memoir. I have done my best to tell the story as simply as possible. I hope it will resonate with you and do you good.

Don't Let the Devil Steal Your Song
Written by Carolyn Cogswell

One day you're up, one day you're down
Sometimes you're spinning all around
He's got you sick and in the bed
And you can hardly lift your head
You're just so down you can't go on,
You've let the devil steal your song

Chorus:
Don't let the devil steal your song
Just come to Jesus and be strong
Just sing aloud the joyful sound
And feel his presence all around
Lift Jesus up where He belongs
Don't let the devil steal your song

Now Jesus said, "I am the way,
I'll stand beside you come what may.
I'll heal your body and your soul,
I'll fix your life and make you whole,
Just keep me first where I belong,
And then no one can steal your song"

Chorus

Copyright 1984
ABET International Music Group
Administered by Justin Peters/Songs For The Planet, Inc.
P.O. Box 4025
Nashville, Tennessee, 37204
Used by Permission.
All rights Reserved

PREFACE

TORNADO IN TOPEKA - 1966

The Lord has His way in the whirlwind and in the storm, and the clouds are the dust of His feet (Nahum 1:3).

Then He said, "Go out, and stand on the mountain before the Lord." And behold, the Lord passed by, and a great and strong wind tore into the mountains and broke the rocks in pieces before the Lord, but the LORD was not in the wind; and after the wind an earthquake, but the LORD was not in the earthquake; and after the earthquake a fire, but the LORD was not in the fire; and after the fire a still small voice (I Kings 19:11,12).

Like death, divorce isn't something that people get over. The broken heart may eventually heal, but the scars remain. The hurt of the divorced is deep. When children are involved, the hurt just keeps hurting. – M. CRAIG BARNES

I live right where the tornado touched down. Topeka will never forget the tornado, measuring three blocks wide at the base, that ripped through town during the summer of 1966.

Afterwards, I walked south from the Seabrook house. For about three blocks people's TV antennas hung down. But when I got to the corner of 29th and Gage and looked across the street, I saw three luxury apartment complexes and a hundreds of homes reduced to rubble clear to the horizon. But now it's all built up. No one would ever know.

A Tornado Named Divorce

When I was in the fourth grade and my brother in the first, a tornado named Divorce ripped through our family. This happened to no one else we knew. Just as tornados today still cause devastation and destruction, divorce, though commonplace and viewed casually, causes the same pain today as it did then.

Eight Words That Changed My Life Forever

Before the divorce, we saw Dad every day. We saw him off to work every morning. We welcomed him home every night. We ate meals and went on rides together. He made pancakes on Sunday morning and we went to church together. After the divorce we saw him for a few hours, three times a week.

> God gave us himself and he gave us each other,
> He gave me parents and he gave me a brother,
> That's all I needed to know about love
> Until a hammer came down from above.

Eight words changed my world forever.
"I'm going to file for divorce on Monday."
From that point on, I tried to escape the grinding reality of my life. But like a revolving door, it just kept coming around. As David Cogswell wrote in *Existentialism for Beginners*, "Ultimately, reality eventually breaks into our thoughts (p.16)." At what point your life may have become a "grinding reality" may be different for you. For me, it was my parents' divorce.

Finding Your Sweet Spot

Believe it or not, no matter what has happened in your life, how old or how young you are, you can still find your "sweet spot" – that "place you want to be," being who you were meant to be, with the people you were meant to be with, doing what you were meant to do – fulfilling your purpose – finding God's will for your life.

Don't Let the Devil Steal Your Song

Our song is our joy of living, our peace, our hope, our determination to face another day, our reason for living. Music makes life a lot brighter (unless, of course, the music itself is dark). We even talk about "changing our tune" when we mean changing our attitude, direction, or words. Since God had a purpose for creating us, it is no surprise that the devil would do all he can to stop it. But there are ways to thwart his plans.

Jesus said to the thief on the cross: "Today you will be with me in paradise." He didn't have time to straighten out a lot of business before he died. He didn't get to do all the things on his bucket list. He just believed and Jesus received him.

Picture for a minute a golf tee stuck in some bright green grass. A hand reaches down and places a golf ball on it. Suddenly someone you can't see swings the club and hits that ball. But the person hitting the ball has a purpose; he has a plan.

He will stay with us for the rest of the course, and if we stay with him, we will arrive safely at our destination. If we give control of the golf club to another, unauthorized entity (spurred on by our own self-centered desires or those of others who lead us astray), ultimately, the demonic forces of spiritual darkness will pull us away from God into eternal destruction. We have the power to choose to whom we give permission to drive the ball of our lives.

There are two kinds of people one can call reasonable; those who serve God with all their heart because they know Him, and those who seek Him with all their heart because they do not know Him. – BLAISE PASCAL

Thanks be to God for His indescribable gift! (2 Corinthians 9:15)

Acknowledgments

First, I want to acknowledge God for giving me life and for leading me to his Son, Jesus Christ. He has provided everything I have ever needed, not only to survive, but to thrive, in a world filled with trouble and heartache.

I want to thank Agnes Amos-Coleman, my coauthor of *Weekly Insights For The Workplace: A Devotional For Christian Professionals* (WestBow Press, 2016) for inspiring me in this publishing journey, for reminding me that, "For everyone to whom much is given, from him much will be required" (Luke 12:48), and for reminding me of the words, "Trust in the LORD with all your heart, And lean not on your own understanding. In all your ways acknowledge Him, and He shall direct your paths" (Proverbs 3:5, 6).

I am very grateful to my devoted and exacting editor, Martha Saint Berberian, who encouraged me to persist in the careful completion of this book, regularly sharing wisdom and insight with me about life and writing. I also thank her for her love and service to the people of Guatemala.

I am also grateful for Penny Hix, who prays for me every day, encourages me to write, and has been a wonderful friend and counselor.

Thanks to my friend Alice for confirmation about writing the book. She said she saw me writing a book in a dream and told me to keep at it.

I want to thank my brother David for being a lifelong friend and encouragement in the journey of life and all my friends and relatives living in Kansas, Colorado, California, Missouri, Oklahoma, Tennessee, Louisiana and Kentucky.

Thanks to every believer who ever shared the gospel with me, especially my cousin Bob Cogswell, Aunt Dot, whom I will not see again in this life, and Dot Patrick-Lamberth, my Nashville roommate's mother. Thanks also to her brother, Steve Kilgore, and Dave Pomeroy, for friendship, though brief, and shared memories in Music City when our beloved Kim was still with us. You have all enriched my life.

Thanks to my pastor, Tim Scott, and his wife, Misty, for love, understanding and encouragement as well as faithfulness in Christian leadership and ministry of the Word and to all my brothers and sisters at Community Church in Topeka, Kansas, especially Bob and Linda Thadison and the members of our home group.

Thanks to Justin Peters for believing in me, Lee Hartman for allowing me to contribute to the *Topeka Metro Voice,* to Frank Kroeker and the band Blues Healer for the great joy of playing music, and Lloyd McDonald for sharing his gifts with me and valuing mine.

Thanks to my brother-in-law, Brad, my sister, Laura, my brother Michael, Mom and Dad, David and Elena, Rosamund and Kristian and Nora Maria, and all my family and friends, just for being who you are. This, next to salvation, is indeed the best gift on earth.

INTRODUCTION

HE DIDN'T MEAN TO RUIN OUR LIVES

"I hate divorce," says the Lord God of Israel... (Malachi 2:16 NIV).

"Have you not read that He who made them at the beginning made them male and female, and said, 'For this reason a man shall leave his father and mother and be joined to his wife, and the two shall become one flesh?' So then, they are no longer two but one flesh. Therefore what God has joined together, let not man separate" (Matthew 19:4-6).

"Moses, because of the hardness of your hearts, permitted you to divorce your wives, but from the beginning it was not so" (Matthew 19:8).

David came from New Jersey to visit right after Dad went into the nursing home.

"It's the first time we've ever been able to see Dad alone," he said. "He always had a woman in between."

Wedding in Southampton, 1945

After serving in the U.S. Naval Reserve on the beaches of Normandy on D-Day, Dad married Mom at the Church of the Ascension in Southampton, England, on May 1, 1945. Somebody took a picture of them surrounded by ten of his shipmates.

Dad described their wedding at the Church of the Ascension, Bitterne Park, Southampton, England.

"It was a cold morning, but the sun was brilliant," my father wrote to his parents, describing his wedding at 10:00 a.m. May 1, 1945. "The church was pretty – decorated with masses of flowering shrubs, including guild rose, pink double-cherry blossom and hydrangea," he wrote. These words appeared in the newspaper, describing the wedding. Years later Dad told me he had considered journalism as a career.

Mom came over from England in February 1946. I arrived nine months later.

'Church and Home, Combined, the Center of Family Life'

Sometime between 1951 and 1957, an article appeared in one of the Topeka newspapers, called "Judge Cogswell Lists Major Points in Rearing Children." The article lists "making home and church, combined, the center of family life" as one of five major points in rearing children. But he may have already veered off that path by the early or mid-fifties.

Peggy, Dad's wife in his later years, had worked in his office in the fifties. She told me she had known me when I was five and visiting Dad's office. David told me that he had asked her if they had had a relationship at that time, and she had said that he was too busy seeing Irene at the time. She had not intended to reveal that, she said. But this meant that years before the night I first heard the word "divorce," Dad had been seeing our future stepmother.

Defined By Divorce

Parental divorce is the *major* event of children of divorce; their life will forever be defined by divorce. Their family structure is uprooted, their routine rearranged, and most of all, their emotions turned inside out. Children who go through the divorce of their parents survive a calamity of staggering proportions.

My parents' divorce defined my life forever. I didn't know how to talk to my parents about it, and they didn't know how to talk to me about it. Today there are more resources for children like us. Fortunately, school counselors today are trained to provide support for children of divorce. Not so in the fifties and sixties.

'He's Safe with Me'

Just before he went into the nursing home, I got to spend time sitting with Dad and Peggy on the edge of their bed, talking to him and watching him smile and roll his eyes. I can't see him anymore, can't hug him anymore. I can only remember.

"He's safe with me," I heard a still, small voice inside say on the first Father's Day after he died. My father had given his life to Christ as a teenager, and though later he may have followed "from afar off," Christ never let go of him.

"...and I give eternal life to them, and they will never perish; and no one will snatch them out of My hand," Jesus said (John 10:28 NASB).

Chapter 1

DADDY'S LITTLE GIRL – GRATITUDE

Gratitude: The state of being grateful; thankfulness.

Giving thanks always for all things to God the Father in the name of our Lord Jesus Christ (Ephesians 5:20).

He's reading to me. Daddy holds me in his lap and reads *Three Little Kittens*. My mouth open, my eyes riveted to the page I just turned to, sheltered from the world on my Daddy's lap.

In my favorite photo of my dad and me, he looks like he stepped out of a fashion magazine. During my dad's junior year in high school, when my grandfather had been urged to run for governor, a young woman wrote a letter to the school newspaper saying she hoped he would, so the girls would be able to look at his son who looked like a Hollywood star. Judges of the competition for best looking ("Most Decorative") man in the Washburn College class of '42 selected my dad. And, according to a friend of mine's stepdad, "He was the best-looking guy in town."

Dad always looked great, whether in a uniform, in a suit, in slacks, or in jeans. While attending law school he worked at Ray Beers, an upscale menswear store in Topeka. He stood six foot two and had long legs, and from the top of his haircut to the bottom of his shoes, he always looked amazing. Even in his final months at age eighty-nine at the nursing home, the healthcare workers called him "Handsome" and "Basketball Legs."

How My Parents Met

The picture window framed the tall prairie grass, and sunlight filled the room.
"Do you remember my mother?" I asked him.
"Vaguely," he said. Later Peggy told me he said that for her benefit.
When I asked him how he met my mother, he just said it had something to do with a party for enlisted men. My mother, on the other hand, even remembered that the number of his LST (landing-ship tank – which Dad delighted to refer to as a "large stationary target"): 506. She also told me that Dad and one of his friends, while taking a walk in the town square in Southampton, met her and one of her friends, and invited them to that party on the LST.

'Look at the Family'

Both of my multi-talented parents looked like movie stars. Mom drew and painted, wrote, played the piano, and acted in plays. She had worked as a draftsman at an aircraft factory during the war. As a youth, Dad had played the violin and excelled in academics, athletics, debate, and student government before serving his country as a U.S. naval officer.
One day I showed my father a picture of him with my mother, my brother and me, all standing outside the house on Seabrook in Topeka, around 1954 or 1955, wind blowing my hair, and everybody smiling, the year before the divorce.
"Look at the family," he said.

Evidence Mom and Dad Once Loved Each Other

Dr. Judith Wallerstein, author of several books about divorce, said children of divorce look for evidence that their parents once loved each other. I know I did. They provided a great gift to me by sharing with me separately that they both enjoyed *Archy and Mehitabel*, published in 1916 by Don Marquis. They both told me about it more than once until I finally found it.

Archy the cockroach, a "free-verse" poet in a former life, recounts stories of his life along with his friend Mehitabel the cat, who claims to have been reincarnated from Cleopatra. Because Archy has to type one key at a time on the typewriter, he uses no punctuation, yet you can still make sense of the stories told this way.

I love that they both liked *Archy and Mehitabel* and that they both told me about it. They had much in common, both being smart, creative, and fun-loving. But this book represented something I could actually hold in my hands.

Daddy's Little Girl

The arrival of my father's bride's parents and brother appeared in the newspaper. Two months after my birth, my maternal grandparents, Thomas Luke George Hallewell and Elsie Rose Hall Hallewell (Granddad and Nana) and my uncle John, twelve, came over from England. Three years after that, David was born.

A song called "Daddy's Little Girl" written by Bobby Burke and Horace Gerlach came out in 1949. I only ever heard him singing it – to me.

Daddy-Daughter Days

Topeka has always had a lot of turnover in restaurants, so many of our favorites are now gone. We consumed hamburgers at Blenders, but I especially liked the Senate and the Pennant Cafeterias. These offered an array of meats, vegetables and desserts. My favorites included mashed potatoes and gravy, cloverleaf rolls, juicy roast beef, ham or turkey, carrots or peas, and coconut cream pie.

Dad and I drank coffee and ice water with our salad while we waited for the waitress to bring the meat and potatoes. People passing by would call my daddy "Judge," even years after he no longer served as a judge. As Judge Cogswell's daughter my life had a purpose.

Essential # 1 for finding your sweet spot: Gratitude

More and more I hear of studies about the health benefits of keeping a gratitude journal, and I keep one daily. In fact, David got me started.

God has taught me to be thankful not only for the good times, but even for the sad times. God allowed them, so they must have been necessary to weave together the tapestry of my life.

I can see now how God softened the blow during the hard times. I think of riding horses at Grandpa's farm in Silver Lake, fishing, eating watermelon and Uncle Kenny's homemade peach ice cream. I think of family reunions, Christmases at Grandma and Grandpa's, Irene's homegrown tomatoes, meeting my best friend at the school drinking fountain in the third grade. Philippians 4:8 and 9 tell us to think about the good things – to meditate on them and that when we do, God will give us peace.

I am thankful for dinner after church at Nana and Granddad's and Sunday afternoons with Dad. I am grateful even for the structure of our life created by the regular visits after the divorce, and for lunches with Dad. The bad times do not have the power to obliterate the good times, unless we give them that power.

Jesus, thank you for everything you let happen in my life. You have used it all to write a story that gives you glory. In my emotional struggles I have tended to focus on the negative, but you have taught me to be grateful for all you have allowed to happen.

CHAPTER 2

NEVER MADE IT TO PRETTY PRAIRIE – GOOD GRIEF

Good: Having positive or desirable qualities; not bad or poor.
Grief: Deep mental anguish, as over a loss; sorrow.

Those who do not understand the influence of old hurts are destined to be haunted by them. These unresolved issues will continue to complicate their lives. –M.CRAIG BARNES

Those who sow in tears will reap with songs of joy (Psalm 126:3 NIV).

In her monograph, *Stepping Out of Chaos (1989),* author Marsha Utain, M.S., writes that if you're not feeling something akin to joy, happiness or contentment, you are probably feeling anger, fear, sadness or hurt. If you grew up in a dysfunctional family, she said, you learned not to identify your feelings and thus probably do not know what you are feeling most of the time! One of her points is that during the recovery process, people learn to be in touch with what they are feeling, which, she says, is a good thing because that's how one experiences the fullness of life.

In church it is popular to assume that everyone is doing great, whether or not they are. If you are struggling with something, you may feel like you don't want to draw attention to yourself. If you admit you have a need, people might reject you, so you feel you should just handle it yourself. But Paul told us to "Bear one another's burdens" (Galatians 6:2).

Dad's Scrapbooks

During the summer of 2009, after Dad went to the nursing home, David and I picked up several boxes of photo albums, clothes, cuff links and other assorted items of Dad's. For several days I spent lots of time looking at pictures of my father as a child, as a youth, and as a young man, with his parents and his brothers, their wives, and his girlfriend.

I looked for clues about him in those pictures, feeling I had missed that during the years after he left home, still longing to feel closer to him. I found out about his life as a leader in academics and school government before he went off to war and met my mother and how, returning, he went to law school, entered private practice and held public office.

David told me Grandma had said, "Glenn was the smartest of my boys."

In 1933, Grandpa brought my grandmother and their four boys to Topeka when Governor Alf Landon appointed him to the Kansas Tax Commission. Dad served in public office from 1948 to 1957.

Born on a farm in Kingman County, Kansas, he would be vice-president of his high school senior class and president of his college freshman class. The youngest of four brothers, my father was an honor student, class officer, star debater and speaker at Topeka High's 1939 graduation ceremony.

After college, he was selected for officers training at Northwestern University's Midshipmen's school in Chicago to prepare to serve with honor on the bloody beaches of Normandy during World War II. And by God's grace, he returned in 1945 to marry and start a family. And when he came home, he became a judge who believed in families staying together.

Back then, most families stayed together, and Dad's divorce could have been a deal-breaker for many voters when he lost in his bid for lieutenant governor in 1958. This may not have been the entire reason. But I'm sure it contributed to the outcome of the election.

Without those scrapbooks I never would have known about his belief in the importance of "home and church" as the center of family life. I believe he tried to tell me many times but somehow never could. Perhaps if he had stayed he would never have felt the need to write me the following letter.

A Letter from Dad

In a letter he wrote me in 1985, when I was living in Louisiana, he said,

"Hi, Honey – I don't know why it is so difficult for me to sit down and write to you. I think about you every day and have such good intentions but just don't get it done. I think perhaps it's because there is so much I want to say to you – and I don't know where to start.

"The most important – and I know you know it – but I sometimes get a terrible feeling that I have failed to communicate this to you like I should.

"I really do love you very much. You are special and I don't want you to ever lose sight of that!"

Drinking the Water Before Washing the Glasses

Nina May Geist, Dad's cousin, told the story of visiting her Uncle Carl and Aunt Susie Cogswell (my grandparents) in Pretty Prairie, Kansas, in the 1920s and thirties. Nina May said that, since Susie had no girls, the boys cleaned up the kitchen after everyone finished eating. Nina May said she noticed that young Glenn, instead of throwing the water out of the glasses left on the table, drank the water out of the glasses before washing them.

It's significant to me that this memory stood out to his cousin. Could just be a function of growing up during the Depression. Maybe I was just hungry to find out all I could about him. Maybe it just explains why he had such soft hands. It's just something I didn't know about him that, when I learned it, endeared him to me even more.

The Death of Childhood

Elizabeth Marquardt wrote in *Between Two Worlds: The Inner Lives of Children of Divorce* (2005) that children of divorce become independent and lose their childhoods, and that this is why they are "two to three times more likely than other children to end up with very serious social and emotional problems."

Childhood is the period between infancy and puberty. But the significance of the term often includes the notion of innocence. So, in that sense my childhood simply ended when my parents broke up.

We still went to Grandpa's farm and rode horses. We played ping-pong in the basement at Dad's house with the new family. But childhood would never be the same. We would survive, and we would adjust, there would even be pleasant memories, but childhood had died. Childhood happened before the divorce.

After the divorce, everything changed. After his defeat in 1958, he never ran for office again. However, he continued to serve and remained respected. He made his mark, but I can't help believing things would have been much different had he been able to succeed on the home front.

"He could have been president," David said, and I agree.

By the time my father ran for lieutenant governor in 1958 my parents had divorced and my father remarried. Until then we enjoyed the golden years: I was Judge Cogswell's daughter and we were Mommy and Daddy and Carolyn and David.

The Pretty Prairie Question

One of the first signs of his dementia was the Pretty Prairie question.

Dad used to ask me, "Did you ever see the farm in Pretty Prairie where I was born?" And I always said, "Not that I remember."

"Well, we'll have to take you there."

"I'd like that."

Pretty Prairie, a small town in Reno County, Kansas, is where Dad attended school in a one-room schoolhouse. I have a 5" x 7" blurry photograph of my young grandparents with two of my father's older brothers, one an infant, one a toddler, standing in front of a one-story farmhouse. At some point the family moved from Reno County to Kingman County. Printed on a card, they may have sent it to friends and relatives after the move. The card says at the top, "Happiness Always." Grandpa looks like Dad in that picture.

Pretty Prairie Question Reprise

I first went to Mexico with twenty-five fellow students on a high school trip between my junior and senior year of high school. According to my mother, my dad had opposed me going to Mexico that first time. I have traveled there several times since.

Peggy owned a white stucco house in a town called Santiago, near Manzanillo in the state of Colima in Mexico. David and I had visited them there a couple of times since their marriage in 1994. In this tropical paradise, hotels and restaurants accent the landscape like rows of curved white beehives embracing the mountainsides.

Palm trees lined the streets, and all the houses had names. Peggy's was "Casa Paz" – Peace House. Both upstairs and downstairs had a kitchen, a bathroom and two bedrooms. Trees in the back yard yielded lemons and bananas.

Behind the back yard of the house across the street, the Bay of San Juan merged with the sea. Across the bay, mountains hovered over the water. I can still hear the lullaby of the tide at night.

I went with them the last time they went to Casa Paz. They sold it for $250,000 in cold American cash delivered inside a brown paper grocery bag. I never saw that much money in my life, except in the movies. I helped Peggy count it.

The dogs always went with Dad and Peggy on any trip they took: Molly, a gray Miniature Schnauzer and Mitzi, a cross between a Poodle and a Maltese.

Earlier I mentioned the Pretty Prairie Question.

"Did you ever see the farm in Pretty Prairie where I was born?" my father asked.

"I don't remember," I said.

"You don't?" he asked. "We'll have to take you there some time."

"Yes, I'd like that," I said.

Still good looking at seventy-six, with nearly a full head of hair, highlighted with silver, his hairline appeared only slightly higher than thirty years before. He had beautiful hazel eyes and an engaging smile.

A few minutes later he asked me the same question and we went through the same exchange and again a few minutes later, repeated several times on that trip to Mexico. In the years since the Pretty Prairie question, other things gradually slipped from my father's memory.

He didn't mean to ruin our lives any more than he never took us to his childhood home in Pretty Prairie, though he often said he wanted to.

Making Up For Lost Time

While he was living at the nursing homes, I often got the urge to call him with one question or another, but mostly I wanted to call him just to hear his voice.

As soon as Dad went into the nursing home, Peggy's health problems intensified. She held up long enough to take care of Dad, but as soon as he no longer lived at home, all that changed. Pretty soon she had to go to the hospital, then to the same nursing home as

Dad, then to a different one. Finally, a few months before he died, Peggy transferred him to where she was, so at least they could see each other.

Throughout this time, I just couldn't get enough of being with him, still trying to make up for lost time, for the years I had missed spending time with him. That kept me going back, several times a week, if only for a short time.

When Dad and Peggy moved out of their house, I inherited lots of pictures of my ancestors, handed down from my grandparents. Looking at old pictures of people long gone became a comfort to me, linking me to times and people from a different period in history – a simpler time, a slower-paced time, a more stable time when divorce was rare.

When I taught college, between 1998 and 2005, I stayed with Dad and Peggy in Topeka for days at a time during the summers. During that time, I got to hug my father in the morning when he still had on his bathrobe, look at the newspaper with him, and eat breakfast with him.

I had not known how much I had missed him during all the years after my parents' divorce, until Peggy let me back into his life.

In between the third and fourth wives, Dad had a relationship with a lady for about eight years. She insisted on seeing my brother and me "one at a time," and Dad went along with it.

"You don't know how much it means to me that you let me spend time with Dad," I told her.

Dad and Peggy became interested in our family history during their first few years of marriage. Dad tried to interest me in it, but mostly I just enjoyed being with them. They took David and me to a Cogswell Family Association Reunion in 1999 in Salem, Massachusetts. Besides spending time with Dad and Peggy, I got to see David and my niece in New Jersey.

Dad's Memory of Mom

One day at a nursing home, I showed him my parents' wedding picture.

"That's my mother," I said.

"That's not your mother," he said. Maybe he didn't even recognize himself or Mom in the wedding picture, but he recognized the portraits I had of him and Mom in the forties.

"That's me and that's my wife," he said. I wondered if he still remembered his high school sweetheart and, if so, what he remembered about her. So I showed him her picture in the album he had put together and asked him why they broke up.

"That wore out," he said.

For a long time he remembered that he married my mother in England after the war, that she was English; that she had brown hair and her name was Jeanne. Several months later, I again asked him if he remembered my mother.

"Who's your mother?" he said.

"Jeanne," I said.

"I remember Jeanne," he said this time.

Subsequent Stepfamilies

When Mom threw Dad out without consulting either my brother or me, it is as if we were shot from a cannon into outer space and had nowhere to land. We went through subsequent stepfamilies like snakes shed their skins.

I remember as a child seeing skins left behind by snakes. They have the shape of a snake but they're transparent and thin, lying there with the memory of a snake in them. But the snake is gone. After divorce number one, nothing would ever be right again.

Soon after we moved to Seabrook, Daddy was gone. Suddenly, there was this new lady with these two little kids who lived over on Parkview by some tennis courts. He took us over to their house to meet them.

Surely, we would wake up from this nightmare and Daddy would come back home.

At a high school reunion, a classmate told me that after my parents got divorced I cried at school with my head down on my desk for two months. I had not remembered that.

In time, I gradually I found things to do to get my mind off the pain – many stupid and destructive things that did not take away the pain for long. In fact my behavior simply took me on a collision course with destruction.

Throughout all this, I lived a double life. Even when I may have looked all right on the outside, inside I felt hurt, angry, and resentful. I hadn't learned how to face down the pain. But, like the children's story about going on a bear hunt, you can't go over it, you can't go under it. You have to go through it.

Flashback: At the First Nursing Home

The first time I found him asleep at the nursing home, I had to leave; I couldn't bear the sadness. He looked so vulnerable. So I just went outside so I could cry in the parking lot. In fact, at first I cried in the parking lot nearly every time I went to see him.

Sometimes, if I found him asleep, I tried to wake him up. If he wasn't sleeping too deeply, he woke up and said, "Hi, Sweetheart," and we had precious moments together before someone came in to say it was time to go to dinner. Then I sat for a while with him while he ate.

Sometimes he said, "How'd you know I was here?" or, "Where are you living now?" or, "How far away from here do you live?" He was so used to me living out of state, because I had spent a lot of years living as far away from home as possible.

I didn't like living in Topeka. I didn't like passing the streets where we lived together as a family before the world caved in.

We had our best times in his room, without the distraction of the TV or the other residents. When I arrived, I sometimes saw a dour expression on his face. But as soon as he saw me, his expression changed to a bright smile, that beautiful smile that lit up my world.

"Well, hi!" he said. "How'd you know I was here?"

"I've been visiting you here for about a year," I said.

"I haven't been here for a year," he said. "Where are you living now?"

"Near 29th and Gage on Twilight Drive, Whitehall Apartments. About fifteen minutes from here."

"Oh, yeah, I know where 29th and Gage is."

When I finally had time to ask him questions I had wanted answers to, he couldn't tell me because he couldn't remember. I couldn't ask them before, with all those people around.

Guests in Their Home

The relationships David and I had with the subsequent wives, and, consequently, with him, tended to be somewhat superficial. After all, we were still guests in their home. We lived in another house.

Memories of my stepmother include boiled corn, which she called "roasting ears," homegrown tomatoes, peeled, sliced and piled on a plate to slap in a bun with a burger cooked on the grill on the patio. After lunch or dinner, sometimes we just sat around the table talking until time to go home.

She was pretty. Dark brown hair pulled away from her face and curly on top, brown eyes and red lipstick. Her voice was sultry and she smiled and laughed a lot, a robust laugh.

I loved her – the "other woman" – the one who had lured Daddy away from Mom – the home-wrecker. She had a name: Irene. I loved Irene. We tried to balance loyalty to our mom with love for Dad's wife, our stepmother. In the end, he hardly remembered either one of them.

During Dad's terms as probate judge, when the four of us lived together on Park Lane, he talked at the dinner table about children at the detention home. I guess we knew that they had nobody; we had him. Then, when he married Irene, we didn't have him anymore; they had him.

As a family we were a whole, more than the sum of its parts, and then we were parts again, but the parts were not a part of anything anymore. Everything that was our world and our reality was over, and there was no instruction guide. There was no one to walk with us through that maze. It hurt and it hurt and then it hurt some more.

Nobody Knew How to Talk About It

And nobody knew how to talk about it. Nobody asked us how we felt about it. Nobody asked us how we were doing. Nobody told us why it was happening. Nobody asked us for our input. Our grandparents showed us couples can stay together like they were supposed to, like they told God they would. And we had each other. Thank God David and I got to stay together.

When I was a little girl and my Daddy was probate judge, I thought I was somebody because I was my father's daughter. I knew nothing of politics or prestige, but I knew I was somebody because I was his daughter. It was a good beginning, filled with promise. I took it for granted that I had a destiny. After the divorce, I became a hurt and angry little girl.

After Daddy left, I busied myself accomplishing things – being good at art, writing stories, doing fairly well in school (except in math). Later, when the pain caught up with me, I tried to medicate myself with alcohol, drugs, music, books and relationships.

Being productive was the measure of my worth. I needed to stay busy, never stopping to feel anything. I stayed on the move to keep myself from looking inside my life, and I stayed as far away from Topeka as I could. But finally came the time I had to return to the "scene of the crime."

He didn't mean to leave us fatherless. He would never have thought of what he did as leaving us at all. In fact, he worked hard at not doing that. He could have moved away and walked out of our lives. But he did not. Instead, he chose to live six blocks away and we visited him Tuesdays, Fridays and Sundays. The issues were between him and our mother, not with us. We understood that, or at least we thought we did.

Mostly, we went over to his house. Sometimes we even went on trips with his other family. But the organism that was us failed to thrive, and in the process something inside of each of us died. Even though Daddy attempted to continue to father his children while living with another family, the losses to both my brother and me were vast.

We lost his daily guidance and protection, the absence of daily affection, the loss of provision and security. We never got those things back. The memory of us as a family will live on forever, but only as a memory, a sweet one at that. I can still park my car on Park Lane at the top of Children's Park on the circle drive underneath the mulberry trees and remember, and cry.

For many years I had not dealt with losing Daddy. I had not grieved it. I had not let it go.

While visiting him in the nursing homes, I got to hear him say "I love you" as many times as I could get to where he was to see him. He would always tell me. I had missed him so much. I didn't even know how much I had missed him.

Essential # 2 for finding your sweet spot: Good Grief

Cry, cry, and cry some more, if that's what you need to do. Just don't sink into depression. At least try to identify your feelings. Give them to God. Be honest. Then be on the alert for blessings to overtake you. I never got to see the farm in Pretty Prairie, but I have the precious memories of time spent one-on-one with my dad before he died.

Father,

Please give me the grace to let go of my unfulfilled expectations, knowing that your ways are higher than my ways (Isaiah 55:9). I release my expectations to you. "For I know the thoughts that I think toward you, says the Lord, thoughts of peace and not of evil, to give you a future and a hope" (Jeremiah 29:11). I know you hear me when I pray and you comfort me when I cry. You will wipe away all tears from my eyes. It makes sense to give you the reins of my life. Give me the strength to hand over the control. And help me to know you as Father in the loss of my dad.

In Jesus' name. Amen.

Chapter 3

LOSING DADDY – FORGIVENESS

Forgiveness: The act of forgiving; pardon.
Forgive: 1. To excuse for a fault or offense; pardon. 2. To renounce anger or resentment against.

> *Father, forgive them for they do not know what they are doing* (Luke 23:34 NASB, NIV).

> *And why do you look at the speck in your brother's eye, but do not consider the plank in your own eye?* (Matthew 7:3)

> *But if you do not forgive men their trespasses, neither will your Father forgive your trespasses* (Matthew 6:15).

Daddy's Little Family

In the fifties, Topeka had a morning newspaper, *The Topeka Daily Capital,* and an evening newspaper, the *Topeka State Journal.* Before the Internet, people turned on the radio or waited for the newspapers to come out, to find out what had happened in the world.

I can still see my dad reading the newspaper at the table while waiting for Mom to serve dinner.

I was sort of like royalty, because my daddy was somebody special in Topeka. By the time I was two I had appeared on the front pages of the local newspapers three times. The first, in the *Topeka State Journal*, was on Christmas Day, 1946.

"Carolyn Cogswell, a month old today, greets the Yuletide lustily in the arms of her English born mother, Jeanette," the caption reads, "while her daddy, Glenn Cogswell, Washburn law student, beams paternally on his little family."

The arrival of my maternal grandparents from England two months after my birth gave me a second photo op in the *Journal,* as my maternal grandparents, my mother and my twelve-year-old uncle look my way.

"Across Atlantic to Visit Granddaughter," the lead-in read. "Carolyn Cogswell, two-month-old daughter of Mr. and Mrs. Glenn Cogswell of ... Central Park, was a center of interest when her grandparents, Mr. and Mrs. G.T. Hallewell (his names were Thomas Luke George; not sure how they came up with "G.T."), arrived from Southampton, England...The Hallewells expect to become United States citizens." Which they did; they are buried in Topeka, in the same cemetery as my paternal grandparents, and my dad, and where I have a plot next to him.

The third time, two years later, in the December 20, 1948, edition of the evening paper, the caption said, "Anglo-American Carolyn Cogswell... hangs a clearly labeled pillow case on her cot, English style, with mother's help" in a story called "Foreign-Born Mothers Tell of Christmas at Home." In England, the story indicated, children put out a pillow case for Santa, not just a stocking.

We Had Everything

We had everything we needed. Dad went to work; Mom stayed home, cooked and took care of the house and us. We ate breakfast and dinner together. And we learned to say this prayer before meals:

"Thank you for the world so sweet,
Thank you for the food we eat,
Thank you for the birds that sing,
Thank you, God, for everything."

We spent evenings together in the living room. Mom and Dad read us *Winnie the Pooh*, *Now We Are Six*, and *The Little Engine That Could*, and said prayers with us at bedtime.

"God bless Mommy and Daddy and David, God bless Debbie (our dog) and Rudolph (our cat) and Nana and Granddad and Grandpa and Grandma." That would about cover it. That was my world. And that was all I needed or thought I would ever want.

I rode on a sled down the hill at Children's Park between my Daddy's knees; Mommy, Daddy, David and me, when we were a family. That was our world, and, once upon a time, we had everything, and everything was the way it should have been.

'Divorce Is Great, Growing Social Problem in Kansas'

One day I went to my Daddy's courtroom to have a different kind of picture taken for the newspaper. It was 1954; I was eight. I stood in front of my father with my back to the photographer, holding hands with a little boy named Rusty posing as my brother. When the picture appeared in the paper, part of a Bible verse prefaced the caption which read, "The fathers have eaten a sour grape, and the children's teeth are set on edge" (Ezekiel 18:2), and went on to say that, "Children from broken homes" appear daily before Judge Cogswell, Probate Judge of Shawnee County. As this little boy and I stood in front of my father's bench, he looked at us, and the photographer snapped the picture. That little boy and I were not from a broken home, and my brother and I were not – yet.

"The marriage is already on the rocks when the other woman enters the marriage," said Judge Clayton W. Rose, a judge "nationally respected for his work in Domestic Relations Court at Columbus,

Ohio," and quoted in an article by *Topeka Daily Capital* reporter Robert Townsend, printed August 8, 1954.

My father glued this article, called "Divorce is Great, Growing Social Problem in Kansas," in a scrapbook, which he left for me in his will.

"In short," the article continues, "the woman is a symptom, rather than a cause of marital discord. It also has been concluded that in most cases when a man is involved with another woman, he has no intention of marrying her and will break with her when he feels like it."

Maybe the affair would eventually have "worn out" like his relationship with his high school sweetheart. If Mom hadn't have kicked him out could they have stayed together and patched things up? Besides the fact that the answer is a moot point, I find it amazing that David and I can still bring this up and it is as real today as it was all those years ago. The article continued:

> If a generalization can be made, this could be said. It is the people who refuse to realize that marriage is a growing up process; those who can't learn that marriage doesn't have to be perfect; and those who mistakenly believe they get rid of responsibility instead of assuming it when they take their vows.
>
> It is indeed a naive person who thinks marriage will turn life into a fairyland. Such infatuated couples eventually wake up to find there are even more problems than before and bigger realities. It's too much for some to take and they hide in divorce, forgetting the problems and realities could also mean more satisfaction in life if faced squarely.
>
> Some also forget that in the merger of two personalities, there is bound to be some sparks and fire, that these sparks, when treated maturely, can be marital strength in the making.

Then the reporter brought Judge Cogswell into the conversation.

Judge Cogswell on the Causes of Divorce

Glenn Cogswell, Shawnee County's probate judge, who constantly must arbitrate family problems, has another insight to the make-up of a divorce client.

"Fundamentally they are quitters," he said. "They have a quitter psychology. They refuse to believe that marriage can have problems and then at the first real problem, throw up their hands and quit.

"I have observed that a person who fails in one marriage is likely to fail in a subsequent marriage."

Judge Cogswell has noted, as have many other judges, that too many people think of marriage as something brittle, that it will break with the first strain. They refuse to believe that marriage can be a tough institution, capable of withstanding almost any pressure.

And in conclusion...

'Nothing, Not Even Religion...'

"Dr. Eugene Frank, pastor of Topeka's Fist Methodist Church, has another insight to the problem.

'Nothing, not even religion,' he said, 'has been able to keep up with today's social pressures...'"

Dad married three more times. Two more marriages would end in divorce, the fourth in death.

Dad's Fight for Families

In 1955, after serving two terms as probate and juvenile judge of Shawnee County, Kansas, my father had come to the conclusion that the problem of juvenile crime should be fought at its source – in the divorce court. An article dated May 14, 1955, reported Dad believed a new division district court – a court of domestic relations or a family court could serve "as a preventive measure in fighting broken homes, in which juvenile crime breeds." He mentioned a recently divorced woman had called him and said a court of domestic relations "might have saved her marriage."

In an article entitled "Court Dealing with Broken Homes Urged," Don Flynn of the *Topeka State Journal* reported that my father had learned of family courts in Baton Rouge, Louisiana, and in Toledo, Ohio, and that they had been recommended by the New York Bar Association. He had suggested that the three largest counties in Kansas – Sedgwick, Shawnee and Wyandotte – should pursue the establishment of such courts.

He believed the courts should take jurisdiction of the children involved in divorce actions in order to protect them from juvenile delinquency. Seeds of juvenile delinquency flourish in the broken home, he said, and the manner of handling divorces is partially to blame. Dad speaking:

> Two people will have a fight and decide to get a divorce. They will go to their respective attorneys and one will file against the other.
>
> The wife usually gets the children. She goes to work. The husband doesn't keep up payments and he must be cited for contempt and made to pay.
>
> In all of it, the children are left alone, reared with no father, and, if the mother works, practically without a mother. Many later end up in juvenile court, and it's too late then. The battle is half lost.

My father believed a family court would protect the "innocent victims of divorce, the children" from the ravages of divorce including juvenile delinquency.

"It is indisputable," he said, "that most juvenile court cases come from homes which have been divided by separation or divorce."

In other articles about the need for a family court, appearing in 1955, my father referred to children from broken homes as children "orphaned by divorce." He was concerned with the rising divorce rate in Shawnee County.

During those early years, when we were a family and he was judge of the probate and juvenile courts of Shawnee County, my father laid a foundation for my brother and me. At least we experienced a real family for a time. Today, many children do not get to experience that.

As a builder of Topeka, Judge Cogswell said the most important element in the prevention of juvenile delinquency was to make home and church the center of family life. But that didn't happen in our family.

His picture still hangs in Courtroom 8 at the Shawnee County Courthouse.

Sticking My Tongue Out at Her Picture Didn't Help

Between when my mother filed and when the divorce became final, Dad lived with another divorced male friend, Pat Murphy. I only remember that inside that apartment on a shelf was a picture of the lady that lived on Parkview, and that while Dad was out of the room and I thought he couldn't see me, I stuck my tongue out at it. I think he came back in time to see me doing it. I remember the feeling of shame, but not much, if anything, was said about it, although he may have given me a look of disapproval.

By the time Dad ran for lieutenant governor in 1958, he was already with his new family.

From Thriving to Surviving

David and I went from thriving and having it all to "survival mode" and we stayed there a long time. When Dad died fifty-three years later, we spoke of wanting to go beyond survival mode. Seeing for the first time what he was passionate about before his life slipped off the path of "home and church" was an unexpected revelation for me.

In both David's life and mine, we find that this event in our past continues to be a part of everything we do, keeps seeking recognition, keeps weaving itself into our daily affairs. The task is not to pretend the past does not exist, but to work into it who we are now and hopefully how it can be useful in helping others. Our parents' divorce drove a wedge into our healthy development, is unquestionably the event that ended our childhood, and in a certain sense defined us as people: children of divorce – or children from a broken home, the more accurate term used at that time.

'Forgetting Those Things That Are Behind'

When Paul the Apostle wrote from jail in Philippi about "forgetting those things that are behind," he didn't mean forget your past. Rather, he was talking about not being satisfied with what you have so far accomplished for Christ. "Pressing on toward the mark of the high calling of God in Christ Jesus," he said (Philippians 3:12-14).

As long as Dad and Peggy were alive, I was still involved in recouping as much as I could from the losses of my childhood by spending time with them, by going on trips with them, and by talking to them on the phone. A semblance of an intact family, even though it was not my original intact family, made up in some measure for what I lost in the divorce.

Baggage of Being a Child of Divorce

Several years ago I saw a picture of my parents celebrating their first anniversary, when Mom was pregnant with me.

"Look how happy they were before I came along," I said out loud. Before that, it had never occurred to me that I was carrying guilt inside over my parents' divorce. That may be the heaviest burden for a child to bear, and children are not capable of bearing it.

Children sense that they can count on the love between a mommy and a daddy for life. When their parents' marriages end in divorce, children are left with a hole in their heart picking up the pieces for the rest of their lives. As Judith Wallerstein said, "Divorce follows a long trajectory." I am sure that everybody feels these emotions from time to time. But it seems to me that as a child of divorce I have experienced more frequently than what I would consider normal or average, the following:

1. Guilty for everything. Every time something goes wrong, I automatically feel responsible.
2. Rejection in practically every sphere of life. Because I have felt different from other people.
3. Anger. Anger is the natural response to having your world shattered, and other things that go wrong often stir up those familiar angry feelings.
4. Depression. Anger turned inward, psychologists say; goes along with feeling guilty and responsible and sad for having failed to prevent a catastrophe.
5. Cheated. As Archibald Hart, author of *Helping Children Survive Divorce* (1996) put it: children of divorce have suffered a "thwarting of life's purpose."
6. That I will never recover. Simple, everyday trials can seem overwhelming at times because of the residual sadness. Trying hard only brings more failure.
7. Like damaged goods. Having failed to learn how to have healthy relationships leaves me feeling left out of what more fortunate people enjoy.
8. A sense of impending doom. Fear of the future. Since life started out fine and then was ruined, I often felt that no matter what good might happen I must always prepare for the worst. When your normal is negative, it's tempting to expect the worst, and an easy trap to fall into.
9. The sense that my opinion is not important to anyone. I frequently feel left out of the decision-making processes that are going on around me. I assume this automatically, because no one asked my opinion about the most important

decision that would affect my life forever, so how can I feel that in anything my opinion matters?
10. Deeply hurt. Deep wounding takes a long time to heal.
11. Worrying a lot. I know. Christian teachers frequently remind us that worry is a sin, so doing so may also be accompanied by much guilt.
12. Inadequate. Never quite good enough at anything. This is a constant battle, probably deriving from the failure to fix the family; obviously an unrealistic expectation.
13. Fear of change. When someone told me that Jesus "changed his life," I pulled back inside. Change meant pain and loss – moving away from my childhood home and later the breakup of my family – therefore, change is still a fearful prospect.
14. Difficulty learning to trust. The most significant person or people in my life utterly let me down. How do I trust the unseen God when the main visible sources of support gave way?
15. Loneliness. This is a big one. The vacuum created inside seeks someone or something to fill it.

I will not generalize every item on this list to all children of divorce, and these experiences may result from many different sources. Perhaps they merely characterize the human experience. Still, it may be helpful for you to identify any of these areas and own them if recovery is ever to be realized.

I experienced pain I could tell hardly anyone about. It was too terrible to talk about. Besides, because of unsuccessful attempts, I kept it all inside. Who was I to interfere with my parents' search for happiness?

I have felt like I was living a double life. On the outside I may have looked all right, while nursing my wounds on the inside. At the same time, I know I have come across as cynical, selfish and combative. Wounded inside, driven to run away from unbearable pain, or else driven to accomplish, to achieve success and recognition, I know I have been driven to find a safe oasis, away from the grief and the disappointment, as life became a series of failures and losses that compounded the agony I was already feeling.

With that said, I believe the divorce actually helped me to be more merciful, open, and compassionate. Because of the crushing and bruising, I can empathize with this process in others. Because the gates of my family were swung wide open, I learned to accept outsiders into the intimate corners of my life. If I refuse to harden my heart to avoid pain, I can be kind and nurturing to others.

Difficulty Thinking of God as Father

Another outcome of the divorce was the difficulty thinking of God as a father. My father, whom I idolized, could not be trusted to stay with me. If I made "issues" of things, he would probably decide I was too much trouble and leave. He would also be likely to love someone else more than he loved me and give them better things.

Therefore, because of Dad leaving our home, even though he did not completely walk out of my life, I felt on my own to produce my own happiness, to provide my own needs and to make my own way in life. This approach sometimes felt like a long, dark road with no exit, like when you pass the last exit to Topeka on the Kansas Turnpike and can't turn around until Junction City – for another fifty miles!

Grandpa's Farm at Silver Lake

After the breakup of our family, some of my best memories were of going to Grandpa's farm in Silver Lake and riding horses. Grandpa had shown us where the Oregon Trail went through that land. Through this I gained a sense of connection, stability, and history.

In 1922, my grandpa, Carl Clifford (C.C.) Cogswell, had been elected state lecturer of the Kansas State Grange, and served as state master from 1928 to 1946. In 1932, Grandpa ran unsuccessfully for state senate, moved to Topeka to serve on the Tax Commission, and in 1938 declined urgings to run for governor (*Descendents of John*

Cogswell, p. 526). But by the time I was born my grandfather was retired and maintained a beautiful farm in Silver Lake, Kansas, where he trained horses.

My understanding is that in his third divorce settlement my father gave his share of his father's farm in Silver Lake, and that the land was subsequently sold out of the family. This is so sad to me, not so much that I didn't get to inherit the land (although that would have been nice), but just that he had nothing else to give. Still, ultimately Silver Lake softened the blow. The land is gone but the memories remain.

How Not to Help People Who Are Hurting

When people are suffering emotional pain they don't need to hear what they *should* be doing (for example, "Pray and read your Bible"). They are probably already doing that. They need someone to listen and express compassion. Some may be able to deny or cover up their feelings or avoid and live life without them. But attempting to live life detached from one's feelings is to deny a huge part of who we were created to be.

Becoming a new creation in Christ (2 Corinthians 5:17) means our sin nature is replaced with a desire to live a holy life. This does not erase all the pain we may have denied for years, and coming to terms with it is essential to constructively moving beyond it.

All the divorces I have experienced have hurt everyone involved a great deal, beginning with my parents' divorce (from each other). I see it now in the lives of children whose parents are divorced. It is so much more common now. These children are heartbroken.

Many experts have written about the effects of divorce with compassion and understanding and agree that divorce is the *major event* in the life of a child of divorce. However, with work, children of divorce can emerge as whole people. Children of divorce may spend a lifetime breaking free from the effects of their parents' broken vows to each other and to God. We may not show it on the outside but we can tell you why God hates divorce.

I wish someone had pointed me to this process years ago before I got into some of the messes I got into in my life. I wish someone would have taken me aside and said, "I've been there. I hear you. I've felt that. I understand."

Taking Responsibility for Our Own Sins

In every life there is always plenty of blame to go around, but no matter what we have suffered at the hands of another, we are still only responsible for our own sins. We can't justifiably blame anyone else for what we do, even if we feel we did it because of something someone else did.

Our betrayers, perpetrators or abusers are solely responsible for their sins also. God does not compare ours with those of anyone else. Jesus addressed this graphically when he said, "Why are you looking at the speck in your brother's eye and fail to see the log in your own?" Still, I blamed both of my parents for ruining my life, and especially my mother because she kicked my father out.

Forgiving My Parents for Ruining My Life

I remember the night I forgave my parents for ruining my life. I was going to lead some worship with my guitar at a small gathering in someone's home, and suddenly I knew it was time. I asked for prayer from the group in keeping with James 5:16 that says, "Confess your faults to one another and pray for one another that you might be healed." We did, and though it did not completely stop the hurt, it made things a lot easier.

There, I've said it. I did not even realize that I blamed them, and especially her, for ruining my life. But I did, and to this day, I still grieve the loss of my childhood and the loss of my intact family. But now I know that forgiveness is the only option.

"Weeping may endure for a night but joy comes in the morning," the Bible says in Psalm 30:5. So I look for the joy, but forgiveness comes before joy. What Jesus did makes it mandatory to forgive. He received lashes and took nails pounded into his hands and feet and hung on a cross until he died to lay all the sins of everyone to rest.

If Jesus suffered and died for the sins of the world, who am I to withhold forgiveness from anybody? What right do I have to withhold what Jesus Christ freely offers? Unforgiveness imprisons you and leaves you vulnerable to torment now and forever. Forgiveness is the key that unlocks that prison door. I know Mom and Dad didn't mean to ruin my life. We must forgive everyone their trespasses if we expect God to forgive ours.

Essential # 3 for finding your sweet spot: Forgiveness

Forgive, forgive, and forgive some more. To not forgive is like eating poison. Forgiveness does not let anybody off the hook but rather it sets you free to live in peace with God and others, and there is no sweeter spot than this. Oh, and in all your forgiving, don't forget to forgive yourself. Whatever happened to you as a child was not your fault, so you can quit blaming yourself for everything. And the terrible choices you made in your pain Christ died to pay for, so you can be forgiven and have eternal life in relationship with him.

Jesus,

When you were dying on the cross for our sins, you said, "Father, forgive them for they do not know what they are doing" (Luke 23:34 (NASB, NIV). In excruciating pain, you forgave. Now your Spirit has been placed in me. Therefore, it is now my nature to forgive. Help me to forgive, and remind me each time anger and resentment bubble up toward anyone, past or present (or even towards myself), to be honest with you about it. Help me become more and more merciful toward others and toward myself. Forgive me when I rage inside at how you are dealing with me or what you are allowing in my life. And please open the eyes of those who have not yet responded to your love.

In Jesus' name. Amen.

Chapter 4

HIS 'REAL' DAUGHTER – IDENTITY

Identity: The collective aspect of the set of characteristics by which a thing is definitively recognizable or known.

*But as many as received Him, to them He gave the right to become children of God, to those who believe in His name, who were born, not of blood, nor of the will of the flesh, nor of the will of man, but of God (*John 1:12*).*

Behold what manner of love the Father has bestowed on us, that we should be called children of God (I John 3:1)!

I had heard that men don't often live much longer after they retire, because work is so much a part of their identity. So, in my mind, for my father, quitting work would be the beginning of the end. Why was Peggy working so hard to get him to retire? Work was still important to Dad even though he was older now. I couldn't even imagine Dad not working.

"He's going to get sued if he doesn't stop working," Peggy said. He apparently was beginning to forget things. This was impossible for me to imagine.

In the basement of the house on Pepper Tree where they lived at the time, all his paperwork was lying around on top of a desk and tables that served as his office at home. This home office looked very much like his office downtown where he had his papers lying all over the floor, in neat rows. He now had business cards with his home address on them. Peggy had been trying to help him close out all his cases, collecting any money owed so they could tie things up.

This seemed bizarre to me, but Dad seemed to be going along with it. I recall going with Dad to a couple of houses belonging to some of his deceased clients, walking around inside their houses with all their things still in them. Every minute remembered is precious now.

Life Went By So Fast

I was shocked when Peggy told me Dad wasn't reading anymore. He had always liked to read, and he had lots of books – about World War II, about General Eisenhower, and about history and politics. In our family we used to give each other books for Christmas and birthdays, dedicated with sentimental messages, our names and dates. I can't even give them away now because of the messages, names and dates.

Work seemed so central to my father's life that at least one Christmas while in graduate school I didn't come home for the holidays because Dad had said he was going to be "busy with the legislature." He didn't say for me not to come, I just decided not to come because I figured I would not see very much of him anyway.

When I was working as a reporter for weekly newspapers during 2005-2007 and Dad told me he had been interested in journalism when he was in college before he decided to study law, I realized there are many things I never got to ask him, never thought to ask him. Life moved too quickly those years, and none of us took time to find out about each other as people. And then time ran out.

I remember the day at the nursing home when Peggy said to me, "Carolyn, it went by so fast!" When the time is gone, it's gone.

Shortly after my father was admitted to a dementia ward of a nursing home, Peggy went into a separate ward and later to another nursing home. Eventually, after about a year, she brought him over with her where he stayed until he died. In less than six months, she was gone too.

The 'Geographical Cure'

A friend in recovery called frequent moves to start over elsewhere the "geographic cure." But everyone knows that, "Wherever you go, there you are." But to me, Topeka was a good place to be *from*. I even had a button with a picture of Judy Garland and Toto that said, "I don't believe we're in Kansas anymore." In Topeka I couldn't avoid my memories of time organized around life before and after the divorce.

A little street called Park Lane and Children's Park near the corner of 6th and Mac Vicar in Topeka represent the only childhood I remember – before the divorce. In the back yard, underneath the willow tree, I played with the kids from next door and across the street. We pretended to make bread with weeds that look like wheat. David and I both remember the horse-drawn milk truck and feeding the horse carrots and sugar cubes.

Our English Springer Spaniel named Debbie would bring strange things home sometimes, like somebody else's dinner dish. I believe she actually brought home a quart of milk once. She moved with us to the west side. But our red angora cat named Rudolph stayed with the neighbors so much that we let them keep him when we moved.

After everything else happened that happened, Topeka was not a place I wanted to live anymore. The memories of the time of "his little family" and life as it should be are precious and pleasant. But I wanted to live somewhere else.

No Bucket List

Some people have "bucket lists," a list of things they want to do before they die. I don't have a bucket list. I've seen the Pyramids in

Mexico, the Rockies, the Smokeys, the hills of Kentucky, Las Vegas casinos, Niagara Falls, Disneyland, London, Paris, New Orleans, San Antonio's River Walk, Atlanta and San Diego.

I've seen everything in *this* world I want to see. I've seen the Atlantic and Pacific Oceans, lived in Denver, Knoxville, Nashville, New York City, Kansas City, Mexico City. I have no particular urge to go anywhere or see anything (except a Mexican beach).

After moving away the first time to go to college in Lawrence, I never cared much for living in Topeka. However, when Mom and Dad were growing old, I wanted to go back to spend time with them. For the three years before moving back to Topeka all I wanted to see was my parents.

'Where No One Else Wants to Go'

If I wanted to see my parents and spend time with them, I needed to be in Topeka. They were both in their eighties. The tug on my heart to get back there started in 2004. After teaching child development in Kentucky and Missouri (1998-2005), my academic career had come to an end, and I had taken nine hours of journalism, preparing for the next thing.

One of my journalism professors told me if you want to work as a reporter you might have to take a job "where no one else wants to go." So when an ad appeared in the paper for a reporting job in Ellington, Missouri, at the *Reynolds County Courier,* I applied for and got the job, sold my house and moved in November 2005.

A year later, I decided to move again, after applying for and receiving an offer for a reporting job in Osage City, Kansas. I was getting closer to Topeka when I moved there in 2006 to write news and features for *the Osage County Herald.* But it was still a forty-five-minute drive to Topeka, even though it was only thirty-three miles south.

The job did not provide benefits, so after eight months I applied for and got a job as education reporter for Sun Publications in Johnson County. Even though I was actually further away from Topeka than

I had been in Osage City, I took the job because, besides benefits, I wanted to live in Kansas City for some unknown reason.

Goin' to Kansas City

The Kansas City metro area includes Kansas City, Kansas, in Wyandotte County, where I taught Spanish at West Junior High my first year out of college. I only remember working when I lived in Kansas City, and that I had a six-foot tall, red-headed roommate. I also made a red corduroy George Washington jacket with green satin lining for David's Christmas present, and a couple of Raggedy Ann dolls, one for one adopted sister and one for my sister, Laura.

Sun Publications provided weekly newspapers for many of the classy little Johnson County suburban municipalities in the Johnson County, Kansas, area of the Kansas City metro area. The newspaper office and my apartment were located in the city of Overland Park, Kansas. I worked there seven months, receiving a second-place award for best education story from the Kansas Press Association. Right after that, they eliminated my position.

My apartment was across the street from Leawood, Kansas. I lived there from paycheck to paycheck in what people told me was the "most affluent zip code in Kansas" (66209). I remember well buying groceries with my credit card and eying all the food items I could no longer afford after being laid off.

A Turn for the Worst

A turn for the worst in the Alzheimer's occurred in February 2008, just after Dad's eighty-sixth birthday. Peggy wrote in an e-mail to David and me that Dad had fallen two days ago and her son had helped lift him up off the floor.

This was on a Thursday. I said I could be there the next day. I arrived in Topeka around 9:00 p.m. on a Friday night.

"You won't believe how he looks," Peggy said to me at the door of their house. Except for the time he grew sideburns for the Topeka Centennial in 1954 and the year he visited me with a mustache in Oklahoma for one of my graduations, I could not remember any occasion when his face was not smooth.

Peggy said he had not shaved since Tuesday. He didn't seem to mind, in fact, he seemed to think it was funny. When Peggy said something about him needing to shave, he just laughed. I had never seen my father like that.

My dad, judge and attorney, delegate to the 1956 Republican National Convention and candidate for lieutenant governor of Kansas in 1958, the best-dressed, handsomest, most well-put-together man I had ever known, was almost unrecognizable.

"Age gets involved," my dad had said to me during that time, in a more lucid moment.

He did not shave Saturday either. Finally, Sunday, we helped him start shaving. He got most of the beard off, but not all. I left that afternoon. I went back to Kansas City and returned the next Friday. He had not shaved since the Sunday we helped him. Saturday, we got him to shave, and back home again I went. Another week went by. Eventually, Peggy said he had regained most of the regularity about shaving.

A few weeks later, Peggy said that some sickness caused Dad to lose the use of his legs. This time she spoke of not being able to care for him like this. She had developed some health issues of her own. She called and asked me if I was coming by on Friday. She said she was going to talk about "options" about "what to do" with Dad. By the time I got there, he seemed much better, or so I thought.

I fulfilled my lease at my Overland Park apartment, living on unemployment, until July 2008, when I moved to Topeka, where I had accepted a temporary preschool teaching job for seven weeks at a non-profit agency. After that, another job within the same agency became available which I would have until June 2011, when I would, again, be laid off because of downsizing.

His 'Real' Daughter

My father didn't have any more natural children after he had David and me. His second wife had a boy and a girl from her first marriage (our stepbrother and sister). He adopted his third wife's four children (our adopted brother and sisters). But as soon as he moved out of our house, I felt like David and I sort of became the "second string."

I was now his "eldest daughter." He would introduce me that way and I would feel something like the ground giving way beneath my feet. I don't think I even allowed myself to feel what I'm describing to you now.

Many times I had wanted to tell him, "No, *I* am your *daughter.*" Of course, I never said that to him. I had nothing against my stepsister and my adopted sisters, and it probably would have been different if I had lived with them. And he just wanted to treat everyone equally and he loved all his stepchildren. It was probably the only way he could have introduced me to people who knew him in his present circumstances without going into detail. Still, it would rub me the wrong way whenever he did it. Selfish, I know.

Then one day, after he'd been in the nursing home for a few months, a moment arrived that has become frozen in time for me.

"She's my real daughter," he said to Earl, one of the men who lived there with him. And suddenly the universe jogged back into place.

We had gone on lots of vacations with Dad. We had fun because we were spending time with him. These were probably my favorite times after the divorce, with lots of memories of staying in cabins in the mountains and seeing the face on the barroom floor in Cripple Creek, Colorado. And we had had other good times. But I hadn't realized until that day at the nursing home when I heard Dad tell his friend I was his "real daughter," that that was all I ever wanted to be.

I certainly never expected to hear my father say, "She's my real daughter," but when I heard that it was like finding the missing puzzle piece. This is what I always wanted to hear him say, and didn't even know it. It no longer mattered what I could or couldn't perform. All that mattered was who I was.

Essential # 4 for finding your sweet spot: Identity

Where do you find your identity? Some people's identity is in what they do for a living, some in their sexual identity, some in their role in society or even in their family, children or grandchildren. God is not really in the picture. But when I was born again, I became a child of God, changed on the inside into someone who knows God in a personal way. He was no longer at arm's length and at odds with me.

Suddenly I didn't just know *about* God or think, oh, yeah, there is a God. But rather, I actually *knew* God. I began to "walk" with God. Now my identity is that I am a child of God. Knowing God and making him known became my reason for living. A caterpillar can't stop becoming a butterfly once that cocoon has formed around it. And when it comes out of the cocoon, it comes out as something different than what it was when it went in.

When I believed in Jesus Christ he made me anew – when I acknowledged my need of his forgiveness, something happened in my spirit – I became his and he became mine. There is nothing like the peace of knowing God, knowing that I'm saved – safe and secure for eternity. Life here and now becomes a wholly different experience.

"He came to His own, and His own did not receive Him. But as many as received Him, to them He gave the right to become children of God, to those who believe in His name" (John 1:12).

As much as I wanted to be my father's "real" daughter, I now want to be God's daughter. I want my life to reflect him; his kindness, his love, his beauty, his creativity, and his truth. Sometimes his truth doesn't set well with people. The concept of sin has gone out of vogue. The truth of Jesus Christ as Lord and the only way to God has become politically incorrect. But people still need to hear it because it is true.

If you have not yet discovered faith in Jesus Christ, I encourage you to open your heart to the one who made you for himself. I can guarantee without reservation, *you will never regret it*. Satan appears as an "angel of light," but he is a wicked seducer, holding people captive, keeping them ignorant as long as he can to his deception and ultimately his doom. He tells them there are "many ways to God." That is a lie. There is only one way: Jesus Christ.

"The thief does not come except to steal, and to kill, and to destroy. I have come that they may have life, and that they may have it more abundantly." Jesus said (John 10:10).

Jesus said, "I am the way, the truth and the life. No one comes to the Father except through me" (John 14:6).

The amazing truth is that God is a *person*. And Jesus was that person in the flesh. And by faith in him, we become his "real" children.

If you find for whatever reason that you would like to believe but simply feel you are unable, ask God to show you what is true, personally, for you, and he will do it. Finding our identity in God is the most liberating experience of all. "And you shall know the truth, and the truth shall make you free," Jesus said (John 8:32).

Father, you have been with me even when I was not with you. You have never left me. You have always been faithful. You never change. You can be trusted and you never fail. Please show yourself to those who don't yet know that you are what they have been looking for. I am blessed to be your child. Thank you.

CHAPTER 5

ROUND PEGS IN SQUARE HOLES – PURPOSE

Purpose: 1. The object toward which one strives or for which something exists; goal; aim.

For we are not bold to class or compare ourselves with some of those who commend themselves; but when they measure themselves by themselves and compare themselves with themselves, they are without understanding (2 Corinthians 10:12 NASB).

He fashions their hearts individually; He considers all their works (Psalm 33:15).

For we are his workmanship, created in Christ Jesus for good works, which God prepared beforehand that we should walk in them (Ephesians 2:10).

I'm never sure whether it's a "round peg in a square hole" or a "square peg in a round hole" Mom used to always say she was. Ever felt like that? I have.

Both 8" x 10" pictures of my parents, taken in 1946, have circular light beaming behind their heads like halos. Even though the portrait is in black and white, I see Mom's wavy brown hair caressing her shoulders. Her light blue eyes stare dreamily ahead. Her head tilts a little. The corners of her mouth turn up slightly in a closed-mouth smile.

The neckline of the chartreuse dress with cap sleeves cuts out at an angle, creating a trapezoid-shaped opening. Michael said the amber stone in the brooch at the center of her neckline came from a stone her mother's father found on the beach in England and had polished. She's wearing her trademark engraved silver bracelet on her left wrist. Her left arm rests on the arm of an easy chair, her right hand on her left forearm. Her long fingers bend slightly. Her beauty still takes my breath away.

In the wedding picture, in front of the church, accompanied by eleven men in Navy uniforms, the young bride and groom are smiling. The war is over. The Navy officer and his bride will be going to America to live happily ever after.

Eyes That Follow You Around the Room

The dark-haired woman with a vase whose brown eyes follow you around the room still watches us from Mom's living room wall. Next to her stands the British soldier in a red uniform on a black horse in front of an ancient building. A perfect oil-painted likeness of Stewart Granger hangs in the kitchen. Every room in the house has artwork displayed, painted by my mother, my brother Michael or me, immortalizing Mom's creative bent and ours.

One year for Halloween I was Pocahontas, another year, Alice in Wonderland. I was a black cat in kindergarten. One year Mom painted our faces brown – even Dad – and wrapped towels around our heads, transforming us into Turkish towels!

Mom made bubbly macaroni and cheese with onions and great chili and spaghetti sauce from the *Better Homes and Gardens* cookbook. For a long time, my favorite memory of Mom and me was me making mud pies underneath the latticed porch at the house on Park Lane and her handing me onion salt to put in them. These recorded images barely reflect the richness of Mom's giftedness.

The Decline Begins

We had a maid named Maggie who sometimes came to help with the ironing and the cleaning. She was white with yellow hair and what my mother would have referred to as not terribly "refined" (didn't use proper English all the time). Sometimes Nana came to help with the cooking or the cleaning. Nana did use proper English all the time.

Dad and Mom and Charlie and his petite, dark-haired Southern belle wife, Smitty, would have drinks at our house. They would all seem to be having a wonderful time, laughing and joking. When there was only ice and a maraschino cherry left in anybody's drink, I would drink what remained in the glass, scanning the adults' eyes to see if anyone noticed or cared.

When I was about five, David and I each went to stay with a different set of grandparents for a couple of months. I went to stay with Mom's parents and David with Dad's. They lived on parallel streets so we could walk back and forth to see each other. Grandma and Grandpa Cogswell lived on Louise, and Nana and Granddad lived behind them on Buchanan.

I later wondered if that's when Dad started seeing Irene. Or was he already seeing her, and that's what Mom was upset about and why she was in the hospital? I remember missing her – like I miss her now – visiting her there, and saying sad goodbyes. Times are longer for kids; it seemed longer than two months.

Leaving the Golden Years Behind

Experts have agreed our personality development hinges upon the experiences we had before the age of five. Judith Wallerstein traces the roots of behavior more specifically, to the "relationship between (one's) parents" during that time (Wallerstein and Blakeslee, *Second Chances,* 1989, p. 120). I have no memory of hearing them argue before age five, but, according to Mom, the infidelities began pretty soon – after a couple of years, she said.

Early childhood family memories include frequent trips to the library and the zoo, feeding the ducks, going to the lake, and making lanyards in the summer. Mom gave us paper and crayons while she painted, made cupcakes with cake butterfly wings in frosting on top for our birthday, and cherry popsicles in those old aluminum ice trays. One memorable moment during an art class at the zoo, a goat came up and ate a clothespin that held my paper onto the easel.

Other than my parents arguing, which I thought was normal, everything seemed fine to me before the divorce.

Between the second and third grade for me, the summer before kindergarten for David, we moved from Park Lane to Seabrook. We shared a bedroom prior to that and slept in bunk beds and David had fallen from the top bunk and broke his collarbone. But I remember this as being the first difficult adjustment of childhood.

I remember the desolation I felt when I found out we were moving. But that was only the beginning of sorrows, because shortly after we moved to Seabrook, our whole world would be overturned, the contents smashed, like a basket of tiny blown-glass figurines dumped onto a concrete floor.

How awful for Mom to come all the way from England, her parents and brother following her, and then have things not work out. No wonder she was always so homesick.

Life in a Single Parent Home

After the divorce, Mom worked as a nurse's aide at the hospital and as a dance partner at the Arthur Murray Dance Studio. She even sold real estate for a while. She did artwork for an advertising firm and drafting for an engineering firm. She acted in plays and was a make-up artist.

After the engineering firm laid her off, finances became really hard. She often said there was "not enough (money) to make ends meet" and complained about how small the child support check was. She frequently mentioned the "creditors." Sometimes she post-dated checks when there was no money in the bank. We always had the physical necessities, but emotionally, that was a different story.

I worried about her if she was not home when I returned from school. Later on when we were in secondary school, she would get in the car and say she would not be long. But I remember being unable to be at peace until I heard the car drive into the carport.

My Efforts to Curtail Mom's Social Life

I did not want my mother to have men friends because I wanted my parents back together. I was angry when she was in the living room visiting with one after my bed time. I sent my thoughts down the hall like daggers, willing him to leave. Until he was gone, I got out of bed, supposedly to go to the bathroom, and went down the hall peering down the hall to see if he was still there. Eventually, he would leave, and then I could go to asleep.

For a while Mom dated a Dr. Pepper salesman. I think his name was Mel. He took us all to the lake, and he gave David and me Dr. Pepper T-shirts with a picture of a cartoon St. Bernard with a keg around its neck. Mel took us all out on a boat at Lake Shawnee and poured whiskey from a bottle into my mother's Dr. Pepper.

Locked in the Closet at the Beatnik Couple's House

And then there was the beatnik couple from Lawrence. She worked as a nude model for the University of Kansas art department and he wrote spicy novels. I remember one title was *Occasion of Sin*. They had a daughter who was sixteen and had a boyfriend. One night Mom took David and me over there so she could go out with the beatnik couple.

It made me feel real grown up to tell the boyfriend I was fourteen when I was really only twelve. But all it got me was locked up in the bathroom with David when her parents and our mother went to a movie or play, so the daughter and her boyfriend could make out in the living room until our parents came home.

Mom's Interesting Male Friends

Mom hung out with interesting male friends too. One of them was a skydiver. He took her to Osage City to jump from planes. That is, I assume she jumped. I never went along to see for myself.

One of them was named Ali. He was from India. One was a local hot dog entrepreneur and one was just a regular guy. Another guy was a beatnik named Larry, but they called him Jesus. I had a crush on him. How you could tell he was a beatnik was that he wore sandals. Mom took drum lessons during that time, taught me how to hold the sticks and bought a set of bongo drums.

One of Mom's guy friends drove a red 1956 Thunderbird convertible and had a wonderful Bassett Hound named Humphrey. One was an actor from England and another friend made me a great big mug with my name on it which I still have.

Our Cultural Underpinnings

When I was in the seventh or the eighth grade, Mom bleached her hair blonde to play the part of Hera, the Greek goddess who was the sister and wife of Zeus. She kept her hair blonde after that, and I put the first streak in my hair around that time. About that year I read the part of Phoebe Caulfield in a dramatic reading of *The Catcher in the Rye,* and Mom got David and me acting lessons with Dale Easton.

A very special memory to me is when we took our Saturday piano lessons from Mrs. Frank Durein, and her maid served us tuna sandwiches and Grapette for lunch. Later I took piano lessons from local jazz musician Forrest Slaughter. I took ballet and tap. Mom exposed us to all kinds of music; Marlene Dietrich to Nat King Cole to Xavier Cugat to Harry Belafonte to the Kingston Trio.

After divorcing my dad and after several years of being a single mom, my mother married again when my brother and I were still in our teens. David was in junior high and I was in high school.

Mom's Second Family

We were a single-mom family for about six years. Jerry was tall, handsome and lanky, worked as a mechanic in a cellophane factory and loved country music, especially Johnny Cash. I was seventeen or eighteen when they got married.

At first it was hard for me because I wanted so much for my parents to get back together again. But I got used to it when Mom had two more children, a girl named Laura and four years later, a boy named Michael. Mom was married to Jerry about as long as she was married to my dad.

Mom had some trouble with that first pregnancy with my stepfather. In one of my journals I thanked God for letting my little sister, Laura, be born. I was already in college the year she arrived.

I adored my new siblings. But because I had started moving away, starting when I went to Lawrence for my second year of college, I was gone most of the time while they were growing up. Still somehow we managed to have a relationship, much more so than with the children my dad inherited that were not really related to me. I have no doubt blood really is thicker than water.

Mom's second marriage also ended in divorce.

By this time, apparently, all was forgiven where my dad was concerned. He was only following in his father's footsteps, Mom said. According to her, everybody knew my grandfather was having an affair with some lady. Back then, Mom said, people didn't leave their husbands for being unfaithful to them.

"Poor Susie," she'd say, referring to my dad's mother.

Shortly before Dad died, Mom said he was a "good guy," that he was "never mean."

"We were together eleven years," she said. "That's a long time."

Growing Up with Mom

I don't know who I would be without my mother. If my parents had stayed together or I had lived with Dad, I might have been a pep club president, a cheerleader, an athlete, a student council member, a sorority sister, a lawyer, or a secretary. Maybe I would care about football and basketball. Instead, I have been a musician, an artist, a student, an academic, a reporter, a teacher, a tutor and a songwriter.

My mother had little interest in sports or politics. However, she loved history and liked to write. David told me she wrote speeches for my dad when he was running for office. My mother taught me about creativity, and creativity has been a great boon to me. It kept me intellectually curious and believing I could do things.

Even though my dad was also musical (he played violin, sang and acted), I always had this dichotomy in my mind. I thought people involved with student government were uncreative and boring. I don't think I even knew Dad was involved in those things until after he died. But my father left us with our mother, so we grew up artistic.

I hated politics. When my Dad was running for things and we would go to political events, I thought they were so boring. The people were boring, and what they were saying was boring. I never thought Dad was boring, just all those other people.

I worked as a page in the Kansas Legislature and later worked in my Dad's office, saving enough money to buy my pep club sweater in junior high. But when it came to conformity, the line was drawn in the sand. I never cared for it.

They may call families like ours "divorced families" now but a broken family is still a broken family, regardless of our culture's penchant for euphemism.

'I Miss Going on Trips with You'

I had this strange desire to witness Mom and Dad on good terms before they departed this world. Had they stayed together, this might have been a basic assumption. But they didn't. So I was glad when Mom told me she wanted to talk to Dad, and Peggy had said she didn't mind.

Before they talked I feared he might not remember her.

"Just be prepared," I told her.

Mom finally called Dad the eve of Mother's Day, Saturday, May 10, 2008 – before the brain bleed in 2010 – when she could still talk. She had been talking about it for months. Sitting on the couch at her house, she said to me she was going to have to do it soon because David would ask her, and she wanted to be able to tell him something.

Michael, Laura and her husband, Brad, had gone to buy some chicken. I decided that would be a good time for Mom to talk to Dad. I dialed the number and asked Peggy if this would be a good time. She said he was in the shower and to call back in twenty minutes.

Exactly twenty minutes later, I dialed the number again and Peggy got Dad. When he answered, I swear he sounded the way he sounded on those tapes we recorded when I was five.

"Hi, Dad, I have someone who wants to talk to you."

"All right," he said in that wonderful voice.

A little small talk ensued. Hello, Glenn, this is Jeanne. How are you? That sort of thing.

"You sound good," Mom said. I didn't expect to hear her say what she said next.

"I miss going on trips with you," she said.

Laura had cooked some morel mushrooms and it was time to eat. She wondered what was holding Mom up. I told her she was talking to my dad.

When Mom handed me the phone, I told Dad we had to go, that we had to eat, and we'd call back another time. He said okay.

I decided I would not give Mom Dad's phone number until we

talked about what I felt was the inappropriateness of telling my dad she missed going on trips with him. I e-mailed David and told him what I thought and asked him to talk to Mom about it if she asked him for Dad's phone number. David wrote this:

> The story about Mom calling Dad is interesting. This is an example that shows how I'm surely the weirdest of the four kids, and probably the most like Mom in that sense ... You were concerned about her saying, "I miss taking trips with you ..." But none of it bothers me. These people are at the end of their lives. They are at a stage we cannot even conceive of. We still feel like death is remote, though of course it could happen at any moment. For them they are beating the odds every day that they get up. If they can share a kind word, reminiscence, an expression of affection, why should it be a problem? I certainly would not feel that I have the power or authority to deny it or judge it.
>
> Perhaps if Peggy were listening to the conversation it might bother her, I don't know. If it was a phone conversation, then it was private, she wasn't hearing it. And even if she knew about it, Peggy might be beyond all that now. She has much larger problems to deal with. She's not going to "lose" Dad to Mom or anyone. And at this point, taking care of him is so challenging for her, really life-threatening, I don't think she's too worried about anyone taking him or making inappropriate advances. She'd probably be relieved if someone took him off her hands. But obviously that's not going to happen.
>
> Anyway, it doesn't concern me. If Peggy got upset, I would care about that because I care about her feelings, but if she wasn't involved, it doesn't matter. Dad won't probably remember. If he does, then it's a great thing. Maybe we should do more of it. Anything that makes him remember seems that it would be good.

"I miss going on trips with you."

How could those seven little words redeem the eight she said all those years before? I don't know, but somehow they became part of my healing. They were the most intimate words I ever heard Mom say to anyone. And they kind of summed everything up.

There were still many scars, but those words came across so tenderly, as an apology, as regret, as love. So much meaning packed inside. She could have said, "I'm sorry," "I miss you," or, "I wish none of what happened had happened." But what she said, said it all. I'm glad she said what she said now. My favorite memory of Mom had always been her giving me onion salt for my mud pies under the porch on Park Lane when I was little. Now it's her telling Dad, "I miss going on trips with you."

Mom said she had a normal conversation with Dad on the phone that day.

"It was wonderful to talk to him," she said.

Reconciling with Mom

For many years my relationship with my mother was a constant roller coaster of good and bad feelings. We finally reconciled and I have good memories about that. In the hospital immediately after her "brain bleed" or hemorrhagic stroke, and when she could still speak, she and I were laughing and smiling and holding hands.

Prior to this time, one day in the early '80s, Mom came with me to a Christian women's meeting and received Jesus Christ as her Savior. Afterwards, she told me she felt "clean" inside, and there was a perceptible change in her. She seemed happier, peaceful, and more relaxed for a long time. Later, she also gave me the charge to tell Michael about Jesus.

"Go and make disciples," Jesus said. I try.

Essential # 5 for finding your sweet spot: Purpose

You may feel like a square peg in a round hole, or a round peg in a square hole. But don't try to be like anyone else. You were uniquely designed to be you. Your work is cut out for you if you concentrate on being and doing what God designed you to be and do. When I first asked God that question in my apartment in Nashville in 1978, I heard in my spirit the words, *"To glorify God."*
Glorify 1. To give glory, honor, or high praise to; exalt.

Father, help me focus on what you want from me, both in my being and in my doing. Who I am and what I do is my responsibility, no one else's. If I am a "square peg in a round hole," then it may take a little longer and it may be more work to find your will for me in this life, but right now I give you permission to show me the way, so that I may fulfill the purpose for which I was created.
In Jesus' name. Amen.

We are here to know Jesus Christ as our Savior and to serve Him as our Lord, wherever He leads us. – CHARLES STANLEY

Therefore I tell you, stop being perpetually uneasy (anxious and worried) about your life, what you shall eat or what you shall drink; or about your body, what you shall put on. Is not life greater than food, and the body [far above and more excellent] than clothing?
...But seek (aim and strive after) first of all His kingdom and His righteousness (his way of doing and being right), and then all these things taken together will be given you besides (Matthew 6:25-33 AMPLIFIED).

CHAPTER 6

GARY PATCHED MY HEART – FRIENDS

Friend: 1. A person whom one knows, likes and trusts. 2. An acquaintance. 3. A person with whom one is allied in a struggle or cause; comrade.

A friend loves at all times, and a brother is born for adversity (Proverbs 17:17).

Before the divorce, I felt secure, happy and carefree. After the divorce I became anxious, sad and angry. But God sent me Gary to patch my heart.

I can smell the red tempera paint, hear the rustle of newspapers, and feel the dry, white construction paper in my hands. We're making Valentines for each other in the fourth grade.

"You were so hurt," he said to me, remembering, many years later.

We were devoted to each other. We talked on the phone a lot. Then sometime in the seventh grade, I broke up with him because of a misunderstanding and didn't speak to him again for forty-five years.

Gary and I had a special attraction, kind of an exclusive claim that was "more than friends," but utterly pure. We rode the city bus downtown and back on Saturdays to watch a matinee, and afterwards his mother fed us milk and cookies at their house.

We used to go to these dances for seventh-, eighth- and ninth-graders in the basement of a church near our junior high; it was called the 789ers Dance. I missed one once to go to Colorado with my Dad. Upon our return, I called Gary. I heard him tell me he had *gone to the* dance with Sherry, one of our classmates I knew liked him.

I hung up on him, outraged, and did not speak to Gary again. I just cut him out of my life because I believed he had betrayed me. I completely ignored him until the fortieth high school reunion. At that point I got in touch with him by e-mail in 2004 and asked him about it.

He told me he had not taken Sherry to the dance; he would have had no way to take her anywhere. He insisted he had only told me he had *danced with* her, at the urgings of his mother. Gary said he never knew why I quit talking to him.

All those years later he wrote in an e-mail that we had "missed out on years and years of happiness" because "someone" had told me he took Sherry to the dance. He thought some gossip had told me. I believed he had told me himself. In any case, Gary was the first in a series of boys I would look to in hopes of patching my broken heart.

One time when Gary and I went to a movie, I noticed these words inside the bus: "What shall it profit a man if he should gain the whole world and lose his own soul?" (Mark 8:36 KJV). I had never seen those words before and did not know what they meant. But they gripped me somehow. They seemed to light up.

They were not just words like you would read in a book.

The meaning of these words is pretty plain, but for a fourth-grader from a broken home, they just touched a chord inside my soul that I would not understand until later.

When I finally talked to Gary, we had both been married twice. He was still married at the time. I didn't hear from him for a while and he had mentioned some health problems. But at least I know he regretted the misunderstanding that split us up. After Gary's wife died, he got in touch with me and we spoke a few times before losing contact with each other. He may have been right when he said it cost us "years of happiness." We could have been one of those old couples that tell everyone they were each other's first love and they've been together since the fourth grade.

God knew when to put Gary in my life and, I am sure, when to take him out. Now that I think about it, I'm sure having Gary in my life helped me get through the divorce, and by the time we communicated again, both of us had found God, so we never really have to say goodbye.

Essential # 6 for finding your sweet spot: Friends

Treasure and nurture every true friendship you are fortunate enough to experience in your life. Friendship is a gift from God to help us through our lives. Let them know you love and appreciate them. And who knows? You could be that friend God sends into somebody's life just to help them get through something the way Gary was to me.

Thank you, Lord, for every friend and family member you have placed in my life. Please cover them with your protection and draw them into an intimate relationship with you so that they might know the comfort of the Holy Spirit, your loving forgiveness and rich, satisfying relationships with you and with one another.
In Jesus' name. Amen.

CHAPTER 7

RELATIONSHIPS, FALSE HAVENS OF REST – HEALING

Heal, healed, healing, heals: 1. To restore to health or soundness; cure. 2. To set right; repair; healed the rift between us. 3. To restore (a person) to spiritual wholeness...To become whole and sound; return to health.

He has sent me to heal the brokenhearted...(Isaiah 61:1).

Society used to call *divorced families* "broken homes" and *children of divorce* "children from broken homes." When divorce and remarriages with children became commonplace, they renamed them "blended families," or "changing family structures." But the fancy name did not change anything.

Cold-case-type crime programs on TV show dead bodies so much we may have grown accustomed to seeing bloody human cadavers. People become desensitized to things they see over and over. Society has done this with divorce. The simple truth is divorce breaks people, and when people are broken they begin to look for ways to fix their brokenness, and all these ways are not helpful.

Healing For Broken Relationships

Children from broken homes understandably may have trouble developing skills in maintaining stable relationships. When I came home from my high school trip to Mexico I broke up with someone who might have married me and provided me stability. But I had liked a boy in Mexico my first summer away from home, and when I got back I didn't want to be with my boyfriend at home anymore. He later married and remains married to the same woman, as far as I know.

God's plan was always one man and one woman for life; a man shall leave father and mother and cleave to his *wife*. Today, it looks more like this: Fall in lust, hook-up, live together, and if it doesn't work, try it with someone else.

Believing relationships fix our brokenness often leads to one failed relationship and painful breakup after another, and usually involves becoming sexually immoral which has its own set of depressing outcomes.

Unfortunately, our innate need for love seems to drive us to all kinds of activities and behaviors, hoping to feel valued. God created us with the need for love and knows that need will not be satisfied short of receiving and enjoying *his* love.

'Something Desperately Lacking In Your Love Life'

I have always searched for answers, and tried to make sense of life by writing. In 1979 I wrote in my journal about a man I met in England named Trevor who told me there was "something desperately lacking in my love life." That red journal is filled with ramblings and cutouts and sketches. I really had no idea what he meant, but I wrote, "Yeah! You!" in my journal, supposing he was what was lacking in my love life. I always thought that about nearly every man I met. Being involved with men was just one way to get my mind off the turmoil that was going on inside. But no one could ever fill the emptiness left inside when Dad left us, as hard as I tried to fill it with other things.

"Reaching out for myself through others," I wrote in my journal on August 5, 1978, "Ones it seems were placed here for my use; and as well I am used by them .... But some do not know that... and, therefore, we lose each other and waste each other's time."

Without a model of a successful relationship to follow, I careened into my first marriage, which was over in less than a year. My brother's first marriage lasted longer. My second marriage was a disaster as well, but at least we brought no children into the world. David's second marriage survived despite a separation of many years and my niece, Rosamund, is the fortunate recipient of her father's choice.

David finally refused to divorce, so his daughter wouldn't go through what he went through. David recently told me that part of the reason he decided against the divorce were some words Dad spoke to him in a telephone conversation, in which he advised David not to divorce. He had actually said words that, if not these exact words, communicated, "I want you together." David said this was a powerful moment for him in the decision-making process and for him personally. Dad had learned. He knew.

This was also part of his legacy to us. He never meant for it to happen, and he wanted to do what he could to prevent the unfortunate set of choices and circumstances to hurt us any further. I don't believe David has ever regretted the decision to remain married to his daughter's mother.

Essential # 7 for finding your sweet spot: Healing

Relationships fall short of our expectations, but relationship with God heals us. Because we were created by God, we find our completeness in relationship with him rather than in human relationships which only satisfy up to a point. Without God, we soon will be wondering what's missing again. And people let us down every time if we depend on them for our happiness. Healing is something God sent Jesus in the world to provide. Jesus said he came to heal the brokenhearted (Isaiah 61:1; Luke 4:18).

Jesus, thank you for coming to us, for being the friend of sinners, for being Emmanuel, God with us. Show me what things other than you I am depending on for my feelings of self-worth. I want to be complete in you.
In Your name. Amen.

Chapter 8

MONDAY BLUES – COURAGE

Courage: The state or quality of mind or spirit that enables one to face danger with self-possession; bravery.

...I remind you to stir up the gift of God which is in you...For God has not given us a spirit of fear, but of power and of love and of a sound mind. (2 Timothy 1:6-7).

The Night I Heard the Word 'Divorce'

I will never forget the night I first heard the word "divorce." In bed listening for Dad to come home, I heard the front door open and my Daddy walk in; I listened closely to know when to close my eyes and go to sleep.

Dad opened the hall closet door, hung his coat in the closet, closed the closet door, walked a few feet down the hall to their room, opened and closed the door. Voices, tense, like rubber bands stretched, ready to snap. I heard these words:

"I'm going to file for divorce on Monday."

As I lay in bed that night, those words gripped my heart like tentacles of ice. I never felt more alone.

Those words pierce today as if it were yesterday. They may have been the last words I heard before I went to sleep for the last time in a home with both parents. Dad may have stayed that night, perhaps thinking it would all blow over by morning. All I know is that before that night, I would sleep soundly after he came home. Forever after it would be different.

No longer could I go to sleep feeling secure in my home with two parents who loved me. Perhaps he would have ended the affair and stayed with us if Mom had not kicked him out. But it was too late for that. Mom's mind was already made up.

That night spelled the end of my childhood. David once told me that after the divorce I became serious and grown-up.

In the sense that wonder and innocence characterize childhood, we both left it behind at that point. My heart breaks when I remember him telling me about the night he asked Dad, "Can I go with you? Why don't you just stay?"

David remembers a time when Dad pulled the car over and told us, "Irene and I are married now," and we both started crying. After giving us a few minutes to process this, he took us home.

Tea and Old Movies Never Change

Tea and old movies never change. Nowadays, movies and news run around the clock, but in the fifties and sixties, 10 p.m. was movie time. On a Friday or Saturday night I would put the kettle on, make a fresh pot of tea and watch a movie. At the Seabrook house, I would sit on the floor in the den with pillows and a pot of tea, watch a movie on TV and feel secure.

I loved watching "The Ghost and Mrs. Muir" with Rex Harrison and Gene Tierney. My mother said she double-dated with Gene Tierney when she was at Menninger's. I also heard she worked at Billie's Dress Shop. Those were the days when many Hollywood stars came to Topeka for treatment at the Menninger Clinic, and one of Mom's therapists was "Dr. Karl" (Menninger).

The divorce contributed to my fear of being alone, which has caused me to be reckless and hasty in the relationship choices I have made. No matter what the basis, this fear of being alone can have a crippling effect on a life and must be faced squarely.

Monday Blues

Mom said she was going to file for ***DIVORCE*** on Monday. And she did, making Monday the day the hammer came down on our lives. Three months later I was sticking my tongue out at the picture of Irene in Dad's apartment.

Angry voices outside my bedroom door, my mother yelling, my father asking her to lower her voice. They were happy before I came along. Now she yells and he tells her to stop making issues of things. Then they get a divorce. They proceed to destroy everything I hold dear and do not consult me at all.

A Question for Mom

When Mom was in her eighties, there were times when for several weeks she would be either in rehabilitation, in a nursing home or in the hospital. She had been pretty healthy up until then.

I used to like talking to her on the phone, but I was unable to ask her when she knew my father was having an affair and how long she knew before she decided to file for divorce. Even when she brought up the subject of my grandfather's alleged mistress, I still couldn't ask her.

"Back then it was legal to have a mistress," she said.

I wanted to ask her why she decided to break up with my father rather than stay with him like my grandmother did, but I couldn't. David said that I needed to ask her, because there would come a time when she would not be there to ask. So soon after, I asked her. It was not so hard after all.

"Infidelity ran in his family like wooden legs," she said. "He was just taking after his father." She frequently said that something "ran in the family like wooden legs." She even said she saw my grandfather make passes at her mother, but she could not tell me more than that.

"It was just so obvious," she said, but I can't even imagine.

She said infidelities started a couple of years into the marriage, not necessarily affairs.

I asked her if they had anything to do with her going into the hospital.

"I was pretty disillusioned," she said.

Thinking about that fills me with sadness again. And then Jesus comes. Sometimes for me the touch of Jesus comes like a long hug from a trusted friend. Tears wash over the hurt like waves of the ocean pulling gently on the shore. The water turns back as the tide leaves the sand freshly washed.

The Hole in My Soul

After Dad moved out, we had to reorganize and keep on going. After he left, I busied myself dealing with his absence and other issues at home mostly by staying busy and being angry.

Not until my father's fourth marriage, to Peggy, in 1994, did I realize how much I missed not living with my father all those years. I had forgotten what it was like to sit with my Daddy in the morning while he read his paper and drank his coffee and ate his cereal with sliced bananas in it.

Before the divorce, I took being with him for granted, as a child naturally would, but when it was gone it left a hole in my soul that I could not fill. His absence left a huge vacuum. His continuing absence in the house just bore around the hole in my soul, increasing its size over the years.

He married Irene in 1957. She had been married once and had two children. They divorced eleven years later, about as many years as Mom and Dad were married. He married again in 1969 for 15 years or so, divorced again and had a relationship for eight years.

About three months after my niece, Rosamund Jane, was born, in 1986, I saw her as an infant. I didn't see her again until my brother brought her to see me in Knoxville when she was nine. In between those years I only saw pictures, because the girlfriend insisted on seeing us "one at a time."

While Dad was with this lady, I never knew whether he would spend Christmas in Topeka or out of state with her and her family.

Facing Up with Daddy in 1992

"I just want to say that I miss you," I wrote to my father November 17, 1992.

> Sometimes I feel that I am feeling all the stored up sadness of a lifetime when I am thinking about you and missing you. I don't mean that in a bad way. Sadness is O.K. It's honest and it's healing. But what I have been thinking about a lot lately is why, in my relationship with you, do I usually try not to go too deeply into what is going on with me in my life, especially if I am having a hard time? I prefer to give you the nice version, a sort of superficial version. And I just realized today that it might stem from the time when I was a child and our relationship changed from living together to visits. It's amazing, because as I was thinking about this, I read something in a book that just made it so clear to me. I'd like to share some of it with you.

And then I quoted from *Surviving the Breakup* by Judith Wallerstein (1980):

> With the marital separation, father and child both face an abrupt discontinuity in the form of their daily contact. Suddenly, they must adapt their mutual feelings and needs to the narrow confines of the visit. During the years that follow, the

father-child relationship rests entirely on what can be compressed into the new and limited form. The difficulties inherent in this compressed funneling process have been insufficiently appreciated ... The daily events which structured the parent-child relationship have vanished. The roles are awkward and new, no longer defined by sharing meals or family tasks. *Neither child nor parent fully shares the life of the other, nor is fully absent (italics mine)...*

The custodial parent's continued presence alone made her an available target for the child's unhappiness and resentment around the visit. Thus, for example, since she was available, whereas the visiting parent was present only intermittently, it was not unusual for children to behave splendidly with the visiting father and to return home cranky and petulant with their mothers. Their behavior often reflected their greater concern that their father might abandon them ...

"I want to be completely real with you," I went on,

"...but there is on the inside a real fear that if I reveal too much of myself or what I am going through, especially if it is something that I perceive you might view unfavorably, that you will reject me. That you will abandon me ... I still fear that if I am upset or have an issue [there's that word again] with you or anything that you will leave me, as I perceive in my mind is what happened between you and my mother ...

After that introduction, I cut to the *issue*.

I had hoped that you would have wanted to include me in your Christmas plans this year since in Knoxville I am only five hours away (from the town where his girlfriend's family lived). It's not that I would have even necessarily been able to do it this year, but it's just the fact that you didn't invite me ...

It's really hard to let you go. It always has been. I guess I just wanted to feel wanted, to feel that I am important enough to you that you would want me with you at Christmas. I feel like you sort of have to or want to put your whole self into your relationship (with the lady) and that that part of your life I just can't have any part of. I feel like, why should all of her relatives get you for Christmas and I can't? ...

"I really miss you, Daddy. I really do," I wrote. I feel like a little kid right now and I miss my Daddy. But I'll have my little cry and I'll be O.K."

I don't remember if he ever responded to this letter, but he kept in in his "CAROLYN COGSWELL" file.

When my parents were married to each other, when Dad used to make pancakes for us on Sunday morning and we went to church together, I remember a Sunday school teacher (pretty sure it was Cannon Hood), as an object lesson, broke a pencil easily in his hands but could not break a handful of pencils. The lesson demonstrated sticking together. It was one of those things I never forgot.

On the radio or TV during the fifties one would often hear the saying, "The family that prays together stays together." I guess we finally did neither. Like the single pencil in the teacher's hands we snapped easily in two. Broken families do not simply break apart. The individual members break.

Before the divorce, we had meals together in the evening. Our neighbors seemed like normal families. We were like all the families on our block that had a Mommy and a Daddy and one or more children we played with.

We rolled down the hill at Children's Park at Sixth and MacVicar in Topeka, in the crunchy brown and orange leaves in the fall, and the snow in the winter. We made lanyards at camp during summers in the park. We had no worries. But the fear would catch up with us after the breakup, and once it gained access, we would have to learn how to face it down.

Loneliness is just another form of fear. Fear that something terrible will happen because there is no one there to protect us. But there is someone there, who wants to be very present, if we choose to believe. That's our part. He does the rest.

In a certain sense, I began to be afraid the night I heard Mom say she was going to file for divorce on Monday – afraid and alone, and afraid to be alone. Fear is like a stalker but faith stops fear in its tracks. Courage is faith to face your fears.

Fear not, for I am with you;
Be not dismayed, for I am your God,
I will strengthen you
Yes, I will help you,
I will uphold you with My righteous right hand (Isaiah 41:10).

Essential # 8 for finding your sweet spot: Courage

Face your fears honestly and deal with them. Otherwise they will just keep coming back to haunt you. It's not honest to say you're not afraid when you are, or just to claim them away by quoting Scripture or staying busy. I have heard that there are 365 occurrences of the words "Fear not" in the Bible – one for every day.

Father, Thank you for teaching me to face my fears honestly and depend only on you!

CHAPTER 9

GOOD GIRL GONE BAD GETS RIGHT – PURITY

Purity: 3. Freedom from sin or guilt; innocence; chastity.

Then the rib which the LORD God had taken from man He made into a woman, and He brought her to the man. And Adam said: "This is now bone of my bones. And flesh of my flesh; she shall be called Woman, because she was taken out of Man." Therefore a man shall leave his father and mother and be joined to his wife, and they shall become one flesh. And they were both naked, the man and his wife, and were not ashamed (Genesis 2:22-25).

Flee sexual immorality. Every sin that a man does is outside the body, but he who commits sexual immorality sins against his own body. Or do you not know that your body is the temple of the Holy Spirit who is in you, whom you have from God, and that you are not your own? For you were bought at a price; therefore glorify God in your body and in your spirit, which are God's (1 Corinthians 6:18-20).

Remember those pictures of Satan appearing as a gigantic snake slithering down the side of the Tree of the Knowledge of Good and

Evil? Well, that is exactly how this false god slithered into my life. I accommodated it in hopes of receiving love in return.

Looking For Love

Wallerstein and others have claimed that girls whose parents divorce are more likely to be sexually active earlier and be promiscuous. Because of the feeling in my *heart* it was wrong, yet feeling pressured by the world that it was required of me, I tried to convince myself I only needed to overcome my "inhibitions."

I had a boyfriend who used to brag about his conquests and showed me their pictures in his wallet. One night he came over and said he was going to break up with me if I didn't become the next one in his photo gallery.

By morning, word had gotten around that he had had his way with me. Apparently, he told everybody his version of what had happened. The truth was not really, but the damage was done. That insidious fear of being left alone – abandoned – kept me from saying, "Go ahead and break up with me." If boys are pressuring girls for sex, especially making it a condition for continuing the relationship, that is what they should say. But I was too desperately deceived to say that then.

Meanwhile, although the procreative act was held out as a means of salvation by many popular publications, movies and books, just as it is today, I have been fortunate, if a bit late, to be able to see the ugly underbelly of the great god of exploited sexuality in our society for what it really is: a sham.

Essential # 9 for finding your sweet spot: Purity

Sex is one false god. Avoid falling down at its feet. It will rob you of your self-respect and leave you unfulfilled.

Dear Lord, thank you for delivering me from all false gods! Only you truly satisfy!

CHAPTER 10

GOING TO GRANDMA'S – WISDOM

Wisdom: Understanding of what is true, right or lasting. 2. Common sense; good judgment: *"It is a characteristic of wisdom not to do desperate things."* (Thoreau) 3. Learning; erudition.

Does not wisdom cry out, and understanding lift up her voice?
She takes her stand on the top of the high hill,
beside the way, where the paths meet
(Proverbs 8:1-2).

Born in 1888, Grandma was always old during my lifetime, but she was beautiful to me. She was thin and hardy with long fingers and big veins on the backs of her hands. She made apple butter, peach cobbler, cottage cheese, and "squirrel tails" out of the leftover dough when she made a pie. She would roll the dough out flat and spread butter, sugar and cinnamon on it, roll it up, slice it and bake it on a cookie sheet.

She did what women did back then. They took care of their houses and their husbands and their children and their grandchildren, and they made everything special for everyone. She made hamburgers with onions, milk and bread crumbs in the meat, and mayonnaise on the bread. She made meat loaf and fried chicken and roast beef and mashed potatoes and gravy and carrots and corn and green beans.

Grandma served homemade cake in Fiestaware dishes with big scoops of ice cream. She made pies from the cherry tree in her back yard. She had a gigantic flower garden. Both of my grandmothers enjoyed flowers. I don't know how they nurtured them or cared for them, but I know how they nurtured and cared for me.

We played Chinese checkers at Grandma's, I remember that. And a hamper filled with cloth remnants in the basement called the "rag bag" held endless fascination. Grandma's generation may have made dolls with them. It's more likely that I brought my own dolls or stuffed animals and looked in the rag bag for a new stole, blanket or beach towel. But I remember loving the smell of the assorted fabric and the excitement of digging through it looking for something new.

Grandpa

Grandpa was a horseman, riding in parades, buying and training horses. One of the highlights of my life was accompanying Grandpa to horse sales. My dad talked about rounding up cattle on a horse in one of his interviews with Peggy Greene. And I have a picture of him sitting on a small horse, looking about fourteen, with his feet nearly dragging the ground.

In my lifetime, Grandpa operated a meat locker plant and sold real estate. He also spent a lot of time at his 500-acre farm near Silver Lake, Kansas, where he showed first-time visitors the marks of the wagon trains where the Oregon Trail went through his land. Dad would take us there practically every Sunday to ride horses or fish.

While Grandpa was out doing his various enterprises, Grandma mostly stayed home, making cobblers and pies and cakes, canning apple butter and peaches and tending her garden. I have seen pictures of Grandma smiling with a fish she caught and know they did some traveling together. But during my lifetime I didn't observe a lot of activities that Grandma and Grandpa enjoyed together. At least by the time they were older, they seemed to live mostly separate lives.

I remember nights when Grandpa was not there and I was alone with Grandma, brushing her long salt and pepper hair that hung down her back. I loved its softness and the different colors, the grays and the browns. During the day, she braided it and tied it up, but I got to brush it at night when I stayed over.

I remember the sound of the train going by every night at Grandma's. It passed by a half a mile or so away. When I moved to Osage City in November of 2006, I heard a train every few minutes, and it made me sleep better. Funny, it made me feel secure again, like when I was at Grandma's.

'Not Ready to Die Yet'

When Grandma was ninety-four she went into a nursing home. Grandpa was already gone. She always said she would outlive him and she did. She was 100 when she died.

All the time I knew her, she went to the Methodist Church. She used to like to watch Oral Roberts and Billy Graham on TV. It would just be on in the living room while I was at her house. She never talked to me about what they were saying, but I wonder if maybe she asked God to help David and me, especially after the divorce.

I visited her in the nursing home during those years before the strokes got so bad, during the last six years of her life, when she was in a coma most of the time. I was playing music in bands by the time she went in the nursing home and I was living in Cheyenne, Wyoming.

I had finished high school, gone to college and gotten a degree in secondary education with a major in Spanish and a minor in French. I had taught just one year at West Junior High in Kansas City, Kansas, where the kids shot spit wads and wouldn't stop talking. Teaching seemed more about trying to get them to behave than about teaching. So I quit teaching after one year. Recently I heard that forty percent of new teachers quit after their first year; I was one of them.

After a few years of living away from home and playing music for a living, I came to visit my Grandma in the nursing home. One day, she asked me a strange question.

"When are you going to settle down?" she asked me.

"I'm not ready to die yet," I said, meaning that settling down was equal to dying. I believed that traveling around, staying in motels, and playing music was all I wanted to do. I wasn't even looking for fame and fortune. I did hope I could make enough money to provide Mom a trip to England.

"Well, you can *get* ready, can't you?" she said. It's hard to describe the emotion that I experienced at that moment. I felt struck by an unseen force. I had not the faintest idea what she meant by "get ready" to die but I knew that something was happening inside of me that was tangible and made me very uncomfortable. I knew an old folk song with a line about somebody being "not prepared for eternity," but I didn't even know what that meant.

Something bigger than me had my attention. I could not have identified it. I had never thought about "getting ready to die" before. No one had ever talked to me about it either. What did she mean by saying, "You can *get* ready, can't you?" What an assault on my addled brain. All I know is something happened. I felt apprehended by something or someone unseen.

Essential #10 for finding your sweet spot: Wisdom.

Be wise. Take some time to think about your mortality. Not in the sense of doing everything on your bucket list before you die, but rather in the sense of the eventuality that you are going to meet your Maker. Find out what is true, right, or lasting. Ask God what his will is for your life. Wisdom was just one gift I received from Grandma. She knew what it was and she lived it.

Father, you have taught me that this life is like a vapor that we're only passing through. You have opened my eyes to the reality of eternity and the literal life-and-death necessity of knowing you before passing from this life to the next. You have made it clear that you are my Creator and that you sent your Son to purchase me with his blood. Therefore, I am not my own. As the Psalmist said, teach me to number my days. Teach me to redeem the time, because the days are evil (Ephesians 5:16).

You have made me love you with all my heart. Whatever there is in my heart that is not fully yours I offer it to you now. Make me entirely yours that I may hear you say, "Well done, good and faithful servant" (Matthew 25:21, 23), and be able to say, "I have fought the good fight, I have finished the race, I have kept the faith (2 Timothy 4:7).

In Jesus' name. Amen.

My grandmother is the youngest face on the top row. On her left is her twin brother, George. The rest of the people are some of their siblings. My maternal great-grandmother, Matilda Schisler, died giving birth to her 19th child, also named Matilda, who also died.

Carl Clifford Cogswell and Susie Alma Schisler were married on her birthday, February 23, 1910, in Pretty Prairie, Kansas.

Five Fort Riley officers named Glenn the "Most Decorative" (best-looking) man on the Washburn University campus in 1942. The men were nominated by the women's social groups. The women were nominated by the fraternities and Independent Men.

Don't Let the Devil Steal Your Song!

Mom and Dad were married at the Church of the
Ascension in Southampton, England, May 1, 1945.

This picture of Dad looks a lot like David.

My Dad was my cousin Bob's Uncle Glenn. Here he is reading The Jayhawk Book to Bob in 1945 or 1946.

Dad looked so great in his Navy uniform. My beautiful Mom is pregnant with me in this picture. I still look at these pictures every day.

I thought, "Look how happy they were before I came along" when I saw their first anniversary picture. Mom was three months pregnant with me.

David and Carolyn in the golden days at the house on Park Lane; ages, about one and four.

Dad shaking hands with President Eisenhower at the airport. Dad was an elected delegate to the 1956 Republican National Convention in San Francisco. That is, of course, Eisenhower's wife, Mamie, in the middle.

Mom still looking very beautiful, perhaps sometime in the 60s, in an elegant dress with the late Smitty Davis in the upper left.

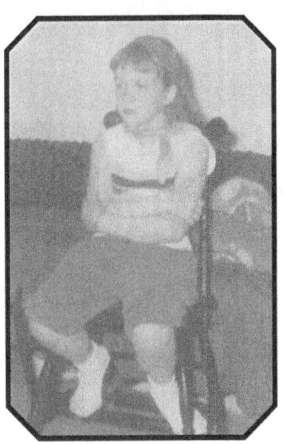

A picture worth a thousand words. Carolyn, post-divorce. At some adult's house; not a happy camper.

Grandma frying chicken. Here she is still in her home at age 84 doing what she did so well: serving others.

My father's mother, Susie Alma Schisler, age 20. I will look for her to look something like this in heaven.

CHAPTER 11

CONQUERING DEMONS – SERENITY

Serenity (noun form of serene). Serene: 1. Unruffled; tranquil. 2. Unclouded...

Narcotics cannot still the Tooth
That nibbles at the soul-
EMILY DICKINSON

Peace I leave with you, My peace I give to you; not as the world gives do I give to you (John 14:27).

Articles in the media frequently refer to people as either having or not having "conquered their demons." This may mean they are or are no longer abusing illegal or prescription drugs or alcohol. The ones who fail to "conquer their demons" may attempt suicide, commit suicide or overdose on drugs. The news is full of these stories.

Interestingly, these articles are not even referring to demons at all. Today most people don't actually believe in demons at all, but for some reason writers choose to use this term to refer to common human maladies such as loneliness, depression, rejection, fear, anxiety, sadness, anger, confusion, despair, disappointment, broken hearts or unfulfilled desires.

People may experience at least one of these, even if only to a small degree, every day. But when some emotion becomes unmanageable, suffering people may seek therapy or self-medicate, or they may think about ending their life. This is tragic. People should know that demons are real, following the orders of Lucifer (or Satan or the devil) who is also real and whose agenda is to steal, kill and destroy (John 10:10).

Why do people use drugs and alcohol to begin with? Is it not in search of peace, tranquility, serenity? To relax, take the edge off, reduce stress, medicate anxiety?

Alcohol

Drinking arrived the summer between ninth and tenth grade. Someone of age had to supply the sloe gin to mix with Coke or orange juice at our unsupervised teen parties. At least one was in broad daylight during the summer while the friend's parents were at work. I remember one where I tried to smoke a filtered menthol cigarette, ate a doughnut and threw up.

Between my junior and senior years of high school I accompanied a teacher and a group of twenty-five high school students on a three-month trip to Mexico. Still when I think of Mexico City, the sweet seduction of booze weaves through my mind amid the bright lights of Avenida de la Reforma, the sound of ice cubes tinkling in a glass, jazz music playing in the background.

The Bible gives strong warning against drunkenness (See Proverbs 23:31-35), but not necessarily against any drinking of alcoholic beverages. But for many people drinking can become an addiction. There is always the danger of becoming dependent on any substance. As some advise, "You can't get drunk if you don't drink..."

In the New Testament Paul told Timothy to "use a little wine for his stomach's sake" (1 Timothy 5:23), and even Jesus turned water into wine (although some argue it was non-alcoholic). Still, the warning is clear. This is an example where God gives freedom to settle the matter in one's own conscience.

Drugs

I lost a step-cousin who was addicted to heroin but later cured in a Christian recovery program. He got his life on track, went to school to become a drug and alcohol counselor and then, tragically, ended up dying from liver disease as a result of having contracted Hepatitis C, presumably from using a contaminated needle.

I knew someone who apparently lost his mind after experimenting with marijuana and other drugs. This friend told me he had gotten in trouble with the law in an episode involving a gun, and later ended up in a psychological ward of a local hospital.

Defenders of pot use – and other drugs – would surely argue that marijuana – and other drugs – could not be solely responsible for anyone losing their mind (there would have to be other psychological or emotional factors involved), but even hardcore users will admit that drugs are "mind-altering."

One time I passed out at a wedding party in the mountains and had convulsions after smoking marijuana laced with PCP. I remember sinking down to the floor in slow motion after filling my lungs with peppermint-flavored pot. Then, as I was lying on my back, surrounded by faces, I heard voices saying, "Animal tranquilizer," over and over, in tones kind of like that of the people standing over Mia Farrow in "Rosemary's Baby."

At the time I was working at a gas station and I was supposed to come back and go to work that night. I experienced the sensation of being underneath the floor of a house, thinking that I would not be able to go to work that night because I was dead.

Fascinated by the distorted images I saw under the influence of psychedelic drugs, I thought everyone should take them because they were so interesting, attractive, and colorful. I remember driving home from someone's house thinking every car behind me was the police, wondering what I would say if they stopped me, seeing multiple images of police cars on the windshield, like in a fly's eye.

I remember looking at my dilated pupils in the mirror and veins and pores on my skin magnified by the effects of the drugs. I remember turning into a tree – that is, *becoming* a tree. Lots of interesting things happen on drugs. Don't think they don't.

Disappointment first got me into drugs. The year 1968-69 was my first and last full year of secondary school teaching and the year I experimented a lot with drugs. For ten years after I quit teaching, I survived however I could, doing all sorts of jobs and played in some bands.

Six Days in a Mexican Jail

In the early seventies I spent six days in a Mexican jail because the police officer said he found a marijuana seed in my compact. I still have no idea how it got there. I could have been in jail a lot longer than I was. The two American guys I was partying with stayed in for ten months, and a couple of girls from Colorado I met in there had been in four months when I got there.

Drugs provided fantasies and illusions. They also medicated pain – or at least distracted from it. I had hoped my love would put my family back together again, but that was a fantasy. So I exchanged one fantasy for another fantasy

But all drugs and alcohol do is put a bandage on the real problem. The problem is still there when the effect wears off. What's needed is a permanent solution. Until we find the permanent solution, we wander aimlessly and drift toward destruction.

Drugs and alcohol have many victims. It is not that people's emotional struggles are demons. Emotional struggles are emotional struggles; demons are demons – real spiritual entities with allegiance to Satan whose mission is to steal, kill and destroy human lives fashioned in the image of God. Looking for peace, tranquility and serenity leads us like sheep to follow the shepherds that do not care for the sheep.

Satan loves that people don't believe in him. That way he can do his dirty deeds on unsuspecting victims who may not figure it out until it's too late, when life on earth is over and they find themselves without recourse forever.

It all goes back to the message of the gospel: "The wages of sin is death, but the gift of God is eternal life in Christ Jesus our Lord" (Romans 6:23). God changes us from slaves of sin into slaves of God. That is where the true freedom is. There is a way to experience peace, tranquility and serenity – walk closer with the Prince of Peace.

Essential # 11 for finding your sweet spot: Serenity

Avoid dependence on any substance that offers the feeling that life is all right, that it is what you need to feel better. Drugs and alcohol may lead us down a path we don't want to travel, or we may not be able to find our way back to where we want to go in life. At best, when the effects wear off, the emptiness is still there. Drugs and alcohol have destroyed many lives. Don't let yours be one.

Father, please grant me your peace that passes understanding, the sense of your presence, and the wisdom to make the kinds of choices that would please you. Thank you for sending your Son to die for my sins and take away my guilt and shame over any and all the terrible choices I have made in my life. Thank you that knowing you is superior to trying to make myself feel better in any way that could hurt myself or others.

Come to Me, all who are weary and heavy-
laden, and I will give you rest.
Take My yoke upon you and learn from Me, for I am gentle and humble in heart and YOU WILL FIND REST FOR YOUR SOULS.
For My yoke is easy and My burden is light
(Matthew 11:28-30).

CHAPTER 12

THE GIFT OF GETTING ALONG – KINDNESS

Kindness: The quality or state of being kind.
Kind: 1. Of a friendly, generous, or warmhearted nature. 2. Showing sympathy or understanding; charitable...3. Humane; considerate... 4. Forebearing; tolerant...

Let all bitterness, wrath, anger, clamor, and evil speaking be put away from you, with all malice. And be kind to one another, tenderhearted, forgiving one another even as God in Christ forgave you (Ephesians 4:31).

Mercies in the Midst

I never heard angry words exchanged between my parents after the divorce. It's one thing to end your marriage, break up your family, and never consider how it might affect the children. It's another thing altogether to continue to speak angrily to one another where the children can hear, or to constantly criticize the absent parent for the rest of the child's life. There were those times when Mom spoke of Dad's unfaithfulness, but later on her saying they were "friends" made things better.

It took a long time for me to realize my parents would never be together again. Dad always moved on, never back, but my parents continued to be kind to one another. I consider this a great gift. It wasn't until Dad married Peggy, his fourth wife, that I realized the reconciliation fantasy was impossible, especially now that Mom was a complete invalid.

The Night They Talked About Trying Again

David and I both vividly remember when Mom and Dad talked about "trying again," or at least my mother had been open to it. I can still remember the feeling of hope around Christmas, after he moved out, when Dad came over to the house for fried chicken dinner, even though perhaps they only did it for us. But when my future stepmother may have been pregnant, Dad told my mother he was "no longer in a position (to reconcile)." My understanding was that the second marriage happened, either before or after an abortion, and that was that.

As Likely as a Chicken Laying a Golden Egg

A few years later, the (original) "Parent Trap" movie came out. I enjoyed the fantasy it represented. The likelihood of children bringing their parents back together approaches that of a chicken laying a golden egg, but if you don't have hope you have nothing.

Children know parents are meant to be together, whether they argue or not. Children know that arguing does not have to signal the end of a relationship. Children know that conflict does not have to lead to divorce. And yet for adults in real life it often does, and after divorce, reconciliation rarely occurs.

Today people seldom speak about staying together "for the children." The idea is only a quaint old notion. Now it's all about personal happiness, with little regard for the benefit of the children. So now we have more children than ever growing up with little sense of security and the example of me-first. Heaven help us.

Looking for Links between Them

After the divorce I searched for something to link my parents together. There were times during conversations with one of them that I caught a glimpse of something that may have attracted them to each other – a laugh, a smile, an old saying. For example, they both liked silly songs from the forties. If I started singing, "Mares eat oats and does eat oats and little lambs eat ivy, a kid'll eat ivy too, wouldn't you?" they would both join in.

I told you how they both liked *Archy and Mehitabel* and told me about it. As soon as I discovered that book I liked it too. It still makes me smile to think they both liked it and may have even enjoyed it together.

Sometimes something funny that one of them would say would remind me of the other one. It amazes me how I hungered for that, about something that has been over for more than fifty years.

I remember times when my parents would speak to each other when Dad would bring us home. They always spoke respectfully to each other. Experts say this matters to children. It's not rocket science. I prayed they would not die without speaking to each other again. God answered that prayer.

Okay. So they both loved *Archy and Mehitabel*. They both sang, "Mares eat oats and does eat oats and little lambs eat ivy, a kid'll eat ivy too, wouldn't you?" And "Snicklefritz." I think they both used to say "Snicklefritz (meaning 'a mischievous, noisy child; especially as a nickname or term of endearment' – Wiktionary)." And, if I'm not mistaken, they both sang, "Be kind to your fine feathered friends, for a duck may be somebody's mother." So in those moments when I'm feeling sad about things, remembering these things and the kindness they both showed one another in the ensuing years, does a great deal to smooth things over and make me cry healing tears and smile.

Essential # 12 for finding your sweet spot: Kindness

My parents' post-divorce relationship taught me just how important it is to a child that their parents, divorced or married, treat each other with kindness and respect. And, in general, it is essential to be vigilant about any bitterness or resentment towards another person. It affects everyone around you and the effect is lasting. Let the effects be positive.

Father, please put families back together, keep families together, and wake people up to what marriage and family are supposed to be. Please help divorced parents get along and show kindness to one another. And increase my capacity for kindness.
In Jesus' name. Amen.

CHAPTER 13

HITTING BOTTOM – PROTECTION

Protection: 1. The act of protecting. 2. The condition of being protected.

Protect: To keep from harm, attack, or injury; guard.

> *He who dwells in the secret place of the Most High*
> *shall abide under the shadow of the Almighty.*
> *I will say of the Lord, "He is my refuge and my*
> *fortress; My God, in Him I will trust*
> (Psalm 91:1).

The bottom, the lowest and the darkest time, took place in a city far away from Topeka, in a town in New York State.

Before the divorce I heard about the children in the detention center that were less fortunate and that my dad helped in court cases. I just remember my father's emotions about them. He frequently became angry when he read about certain crimes in the newspaper. I remember one such time. He read something in the paper and then put it down on the table and started saying things I could not follow.

"What did he do?" I asked.

"He raped a girl," he said. This made him really mad. I didn't even know what meant.

Don't Let the Devil Steal Your Song!

I didn't even know where babies came from. When I asked my dad where I came from he told me he and Mommy prayed to have a little girl.

In 1969 JFK was dead, Bobby Kennedy was dead, and Martin Luther King Jr. was dead. Soon after my year teaching Spanish in Kansas City, Kansas, I was looking for love and, I thought, enlightenment. I gave in to the illusion of love and imagined that drugs "expanded my mind."

"Turn on, tune in, drop out," Timothy Leary said. Among the university set, using drugs was considered fashionable and smart, exciting and adventurous, a "spiritual" discovery. It made all the big magazines with full color spreads of pictures mimicking the drug-induced pictures inside people's heads.

Somehow I got the idea that some drug dealer I met one summer wanted me to follow him to his home town in another state. So I saved up some money from my factory job and bought a bus ticket. When I surprised my friend by arriving on a bus, he had a surprise for me. He was living with his mother, selling insurance, and was not in a position to take me in. Goodbye, click. So, there I was, literally on the street.

And his home town had more surprises for me. Someone I met in a bar offered me shelter for a few days. I remember nothing about the person, nothing about the place or how long I stayed. I just remember talking to the owner of a cigar shop in a mall to let me draw pastel portraits out of his shop.

In the mall a good-looking, smooth-talking, well-dressed man started talking to me and making a huge fuss over me. I think he sat for me while I drew his pastel portrait. He seemed to know I wasn't making enough money to live on. He seemed nice. He had another idea about how I could make money.

Hanging out with these people was like getting initiated into a secret society, this little enclave of admiring groupies who were all providing income for this guy. By the grace of God I escaped in time from this situation. I packed my things and left Mr. Smooth Talker with very little resistance.

Next, I answered an ad in the paper for dancers and started dancing in a bar. The money was not too bad for doing something so fun and easy.

At closing time one cold, snowy night, two men offered me a ride home. I assumed they were friends of one of the dancers, because they had been talking to her all night at the bar. I got in a car with them but they did not take me home. They took me to some house and raped me. When I tried to escape one of them held a gun to my head. Afterwards, I grabbed my purse and ran out of the house. Although I had been paid $90 that night, there was no money in my purse.

I decided to flag down a taxi, but not before these two guys came up in the car and offered to take me home. I kept running. I ran out in the middle of the street to stop the taxi. I had no idea where I was. When I got in the taxi I told the driver what had happened to me, and that I had no money. I told him where I lived and he took me home. God bless that taxi driver, wherever he is.

When I got to where I was living with my boyfriend, he was waiting up for me. Before I could explain anything, he slapped me across the face. That was the first and last time. The next day I left the boyfriend and found a room to rent. I must have worked a week or two, long enough to get bus fare back to Kansas.

There was no medical exam, no reporting of a crime, but there is no mystery about why I did not report it. Why expose myself to more shame and embarrassment? Who would believe me? Someone was looking out for me. That's all I know.

Essential # 13 for finding your sweet spot: Protection

I had certainly not done anything to merit God's protection at this point in my life. But you cannot convince me that God is not real and that he did not in a very definite way protect me during that period of my life. So, no matter where you are, or no matter where someone is that you care about and are concerned about, know that God cares for them even more than you do. And God cares about you. God's amazing grace (unmerited favor) is the only way I know how to explain why I am still here today.

Jesus, there is nowhere that you are not. But I don't always remember. Please help me remember to look for you when the way seems dark. You have been there for me in my darkest night and brought me to your banqueting table despite my ignorance. You went all the way to the cross for me and you will never leave or forsake me. I did nothing to deserve your protection, your favor, your mercy, your blessing, your amazing grace or your presence. But because you are God and know all things, you honored your plan for my life in spite of me. Thank You.

Chapter 14

A PLACE YOU DON'T WANT TO GO – HUMILITY

Humility 1. The quality or condition of being humble; lack of pride.

Humble 1. Marked by meekness or modesty in behavior, attitude or spirit.

The wicked shall be turned into hell, and all the nations that forget God (Psalm 9:17).

I would have far more fear of being mistaken, and of finding that the Christian religion was true, than of not being mistaken in believing it true. BLAISE PASCAL

The word "pride" in the Bible is not the same as in English. In English it's about self-respect or feeling good about an accomplishment. In the Hebrew and Greek it has more to do with arrogance, or presumption, usually with respect to God. In the same way, meekness or humility does not refer to having low self-esteem, but rather knowing that you are not greater than God. Concepts like hell, though not pleasant, are addressed in the Bible, which Jesus frequently quoted, and he made numerous references to hell.

Denying its existence and dismissing our deserving to go there would be pride, the opposite of humility.

Imagine a place without God. No light, no beauty, no love, no mercy. Jesus Christ spoke of eternity without God as a place of "outer darkness," a "furnace of fire," "weeping and gnashing of teeth (Matthew 8:12; 13:42; 22:13; 24:51; 25:30; Luke 13:28).

The Bible also speaks of the furnace (Matthew 13:42) or "lake of fire burning with brimstone" created for the devil and his angels but where people will end up who die without making things right with God (Revelation 19:20; 20:10,14,15; 21:8).

Jesus spoke often of a place of "weeping and gnashing of teeth," a figure of speech denoting utter hopelessness and anguish. He undoubtedly believed that those who rejected salvation by grace through faith in his atoning death and resurrection would spend eternity there.

In 1975 I had not given much thought at all to heaven and hell. I had simply decided to embark on my plan B to find my sweet spot, since becoming a Spanish teacher had not worked out.

I had decided to take art classes at Kansas University. I was living with friends in Lawrence, Kansas, so I just went to classes and partied with my friends, not thinking much about God, even though, while living in Lawrence, I did meet "Aunt Dot," the mother of a boy I was dating, who talked to me about Jesus whenever I saw her.

One night I experienced a dream that was simply too real. Diseased and disfigured human forms like corpses wandered around aimlessly on what looked like the surface of the moon. As the horrible figures approached, they appeared not to see me and I had to move out of the way so they would not walk into me. One looked like an old woman with one huge bulging eye and open sores on her face. Her voice groaned in a low, hoarse moan.

In something like a jungle in the background I heard the sounds of guns firing and knives plunging into the flesh and bones of those who were unable to escape. All these creatures seemed to be fighting each other. I lay down on the ground and waited until I felt like I could run. I had never felt so full of fear in my life.

Then I started running blindly, screaming. Back in the street, I passed the old woman with the bulging eye. When I saw her I screamed again, and found myself on my back, gripping the floor with the palms of my hands, my heart beating wildly. I must have awakened myself screaming.

The moonlight shining in the sky never looked so beautiful. The peaceful darkness of that night was the sweetest moment of my life. My chest had that congested feeling of being unable to catch my breath. I struggled to fill my lungs, and, as I exhaled, I breathed two words:

"Thank you," I said aloud. Never had I meant anything more.

The memory of that experience lingered. It disturbed me. The horrible sight, sounds, and feel of that place have never left me. Whether or not the place of my dream was the actual place described in the Bible, I woke up from that dream convinced that there is a place such as the one Jesus spoke of, and grateful that I was not there. I saw and experienced a place that was certainly hell-like, and I don't want anybody to go there or anywhere like it.

I also know from that experience that heaven cannot be a place where everyone goes, no matter how they lived their life on earth. Those creatures there were human-like, and they were in torment. Most people seem to think that everyone goes to "a better place" because God is a loving God. But now I am totally convinced there is another place that is not "better." God is almighty and awesome and holy and we should not take chances with our eternal destiny.

People seem to be willing to believe anything but the Bible. For example, these people that have themselves frozen trusting that science will figure out a way to raise them to life again, maybe even in 100 years. But they refuse to believe in a God who commands reverence and provided a way for people to live forever. Even people who don't believe in Jesus seem to admire him. And he believed in the Bible. He quoted it all the time.

The devil wants everyone to believe there is no final judgment for sinners, and therefore, everyone must go to heaven. But the Bible teaches that heaven is a place where everybody loves God and has believed in Jesus Christ, their sins forgiven and the Holy Spirit living in them. That way God can see Christ in them and accept them.

Of course, people can choose to believe there is no God and no judgment for sinners, judge themselves as "no worse than those churchgoers," and think their judgment is better than God's, but I'm with Pascal: I'd rather be wrong about believing it to be true than wrong about believing it to be not true. It's not worth losing your soul for eternity.

Christ gave the command to warn others of God's judgment. Jesus actually said we were "condemned already" (John 3:18). I cannot verify that what I saw in my dream was a picture of the real place or just a warning in the form of a dream, but regardless, the Scripture is clear. "It is appointed for men to die once, but after this the judgment" (Hebrews 9:27).

Essential # 14 for finding your sweet spot: Humility

God sent Jesus to be our sacrifice for sin. And he gives us a choice: Life or death. Jesus taught that if we choose to repent of our sin and stay humble before God, our lives will be blessed and our eternity secure. If, instead, we continue to resist God's love, we will spend our lives and eternity without God and end up in a place of weeping and gnashing of teeth.

God's perfect justice requires punishment, and he even provided the perfect sacrifice for sin in his own Son. All that is left for us to do is to receive this free gift. There are many mysteries to be found in God, but they do not include the need for repentance, God's incarnation in Jesus Christ, his crucifixion, his resurrection, his presence in the world seeking to save sinners, and that there was something called sin he came to save us from.

Father, in Jesus' name, please make the reality of final judgment for sin and eternity with God for repentant sinners present in my mind and life, so I can make wise choices with what time I have left on earth.

In Jesus' name. Amen.

CHAPTER 15

A DIFFERENT KIND OF HIGH – SALVATION

Salvation: 2. a. *Theol.* The deliverance of man or his soul from the power or penalty of sin; redemption.

For God so loved the world that He gave His only begotten Son, that whoever believes in Him should not perish but have everlasting life (John 3:16).

On July 1, 1971, while I was working in a hot springs restaurant in Idaho Springs, Colorado, a young fellow with a shock of yellow hair approached me.

"Jesus loves you," he said.

"I'm glad *somebody* does," I said. Two weeks before, he had been addicted to heroin, he said, but Jesus had saved him and cured him of his addiction. He invited me to church.

So I went with him to a church in Denver where everybody held red songbooks, sang real loud and clapped. That night I understood for the first time that *I* needed a savior and that Jesus had died for *my* sins.

After going to the altar and talking to some counselors afterwards, my new friend and I went around the streets with a group of other believers "witnessing" door to door. I felt something like being high while I was with these people – loved, euphoric, peaceful, and happy. Later on that night, my new friend's behavior reflected the values he had before Christ had saved him. So I threw him out of my home and never saw him again. Then I began to believe that all so-called "born-again" Christians were a bunch of hypocrites, and did not enter a church again until 1978.

A warm feeling washed over me when I ran across my friend's little note scrawled in the little white Bible he gave me the night he took me to church, and I forgave him for what happened afterwards. I understand now that God sent him to tell me that Jesus loved me. I know because the same thing has happened to me many times. Usually people ignore me. Sometimes they say thank you. One person said, "He loves you too." You never know how a person will respond.

Essential # 15 for finding your sweet spot: Salvation

The message is so simple a child can understand it, yet we grownups wrestle so much with the reality of God's love demonstrated to us on the cross and in Christ's resurrection and continued presence in the world through the Holy Spirit. The sooner we become willing to see that we are sinners in need of a savior the sooner we can begin to live the life for which we were created and one that honors God. The truth is Jesus does love you. This is not just something quaint to say.

Dear Jesus,
You laid down your life for me, so that I would not die in my sins. You gave yourself for me. Therefore, my life is no longer my own; it is yours. If my heart is divided and not completely yours, please deal with me in order that I may be prepared for eternity and that others may see your life in me.
I'm asking in your name. Amen.

Chapter 16

LOVES THAT DON'T LOVE BACK – LOVE GOD

Love: 8.a. God's benevolence and mercy toward man. b. Man's devotion to or adoration of God. c. The feeling of benevolence, kindness or brotherhood toward others.

"...do you love me more than these?" (John 21:15)

I lulled myself to sleep singing "I love you" to God, at nap time, lying on my bed, looking out the window. I notice little children don't have any trouble believing in God, unless they've been taught not to. But if they grow up and are not taught to love God, they learn to love other things instead, loves that that don't love back.

Art

Having grown up with a painter and having used art materials since early childhood, I naturally grew up enjoying drawing and painting. But art, although a longstanding love interest, eventually proved unworthy of a lifetime of devotion. I did portrait drawings at a couple of church fairs and at a tobacco shop in New York State, and I sold a couple of paintings at a park in Baton Rouge. I studied drawing and painting at Kansas University for a couple of years, exhibited a painting in a student exhibit there, and had the offer of an art scholarship but turned it down to play music. I loved art but art didn't love me back.

Music

In 1976, during the second year I was studying art at KU, David had met an all-girl band on the road and had gotten them in touch with me, so I arranged to take off during spring break to audition at a Ramada Inn in Rochester, Minnesota.

I was nervous. I sang and played "Silver Threads and Golden Needles" and "Your Cheatin' Heart." Helen, the band leader, sent me home with some tapes to learn their songs. She said she didn't need a piano player right then, but when she did, she'd call me.

Cheyenne

A few weeks later, I got a call from a woman named Shirley in Cheyenne, Wyoming. She said that Helen had told her I could do the job, so two weeks before the end of Spring semester, I quit art classes and went to Cheyenne to play piano and sing in Shirley's band. My thinking was art is great, but music is so *immediate*.

By now I believed music was my life. Sometimes we went on the road; sometimes we stayed at home. We played five sets a night, six nights a week. When in town we had all-day practices. Shirley cooked chicken and mashed potatoes and gravy and we drank coffee and practiced all day long. What I miss most about playing professionally is the community it created. It has never since been duplicated.

Nashville

Later, in Nashville, I talked to one agent who was offering me a singing job at a hotel. I would be the "sex symbol for the hotel," he said. Oh, good, just what I always wanted.

"You *are* a country artist, aren't you?" asked another, as if there were no other way a musician could work and live in that town. I had never labeled myself a "country artist," even though I may have sounded like one.

I played xylophone on a car commercial once for $30. I played piano on a demo and sang on another. I played on the road with a band for five months. All of this was great fun. But I was looking for something else – could not tell you what at the time – that something missing, that I had to keep pursuing until I found it.

On the road I met musicians who were using drugs and cheating on their wives while pursuing their chosen profession. Some of them even preached to me and, while smoking pot, sang me gospel songs they had written. I had been happy playing music in Cheyenne and on the road, and I had played music on the road out of Nashville, but there was still something missing. Music did not love me back either.

Romance

My first marriage only lasted ten months, but we kept in touch for many years after our divorce. The second one lasted less than three years including a long separation.

I entered into both of my marriages with very little preparation. The simplest explanation for why they failed? In both of them, we were not prepared to love unselfishly. I only knew how to fall in love with love, and I didn't know relationships did not heal loneliness.

After my first divorce, I moved home for a while, then decided to go to Nashville, where my ex-husband had recently moved. I will always associate the smell of honeysuckle with that moment in time when we tried to get together again but it didn't work.

A Funny Thing about Honeysuckle

It's a funny thing about honeysuckle. I used to think I wanted some growing in my yard because of the fragrance flowing from flowers that look and smell like little wild gardenias. When I owned a house in Missouri, I found out you don't have to buy honeysuckle. Honeysuckle seems to spontaneously generate. Blooms appear out of nowhere and wrap their roots around everything. You have to go to great lengths to get rid of honeysuckle.

One day in my garden I discovered that honeysuckle has roots like tentacles. Maybe honeysuckle is a metaphor for my relationship with my first husband. Until a few years ago, we still contacted each other for one thing or another, and we saw each other a couple of times. But even though I remained attached to him, I knew it would take more than emotional attachment to create a marriage.

From the moment I became a follower of Jesus, I wanted God to "heal our marriage" and prayed to that effect, but God did not answer that prayer. That never extinguished the feelings I had for him, but our lives are very different. My cousin Bob told me a long time ago I would never forget that relationship. I don't know how he knew.

After we tried to get back together in Nashville in 1978, he moved to another city in another state, and I moved into his old apartment. That was where I asked God what my purpose was.

First Lessons in God's Ways

Trying to find God when you don't even know what you're looking for can be quite an adventure. When I first arrived in Nashville, I got a job selling encyclopedias door to door and met Kim, my future roommate. God used Kim's mother, whose name was also Dot, like Aunt Dot in Lawrence, to help steer me to Jesus. That's how my story became a "Dot to Dot" testimony.

Kim's mother told me there were other things to do in life besides the music business. That had never crossed my mind. I did not believe there was anything worth doing in the world besides playing music. She also spoke to me about the necessity for salvation.

I had written a poem about Thanksgiving and expressed my views about being thankful to God, "or whatever you call him," I wrote, "Allah or whatever." She didn't criticize me; she just asked me if I had a Bible and I said no. So she went and found one, a little black Gideon's Bible she had thrown away. The cover was kind of worn and beginning to mold.

I thought later that was a pretty good metaphor for how Jesus saved me. Later, I could see how, by trying to live independently from God, I had been throwing my life away, and Jesus had pulled me out of the trashcan just like Dot had pulled that Bible out of the waste basket.

Shortly after Dot gave me the little Gideon's Bible, I was out running around doing who knows what, and I had been smoking pot, so I was a little high. I think I was arriving home, and under the porch light I got the urge to pull the little Bible out of my purse and see what it would say. The following verse popped out, as if framed in neon lights:

"That we henceforth be no more children, tossed to and fro and carried about with every wind of doctrine, by the sleight of men, and cunning craftiness, whereby they lie in wait to deceive" (Ephesians 4:14 KJV). I believe God was telling me not to be deceived by pleasant sounding sayings, because if they don't point to Jesus, they are simply tossing me about like a leaf in the wind.

Still in Nashville, sometime in 1978, I heard a still, small voice say these words to me:

"You believe in things you cannot see: emotions, thoughts, abstract concepts. In the same way, there is life beyond this life." It sounded like Jesus to me. By now I was thirty-two.

A Butterfly on the Highway

Still in Nashville, I was driving on highway 66 on the way home from a job interview. I had on a flowered skirt, with the colors of aquamarine blue, spring green, magenta, black and yellow. I was driving my white Ford Econoline van and smoking a marijuana cigarette. Suddenly I heard a thump; something hit the wing of the van and sailed in the window. I looked down and a big, beautiful butterfly had landed on my orange shag-carpeted engine cover and slowly flapped its wings until it died.

I cried as I watched it die and God awoke something inside me. As I was looking at it, I noticed the colors. They were the same as the ones I was wearing. I believe God was telling me I was going the wrong way – that I was in danger, like a butterfly on the highway. It seemed like I could never escape that butterfly on the highway metaphor. I decided to get out of Nashville.

First Attempts at Going to Church

Before I left, Kim took me to her mother's church where I saw things I did not see in the denomination I grew up in or any other church I had ever been to. People cried and got up out of the pews and walked down the aisles and knelt at the altar in front of everybody! As strange as this appeared to me, I could not escape the warm feeling in the room while all this was going on, the undeniable presence of the Holy Spirit and the love of God.

One of the guys in the band I had played in said I might meet the kind of man I was looking for in church. When I decided to start going to church, I went to a church more like the one I had been raised in. There I met a married man who, after a couple of conversations, decided he was going to leave his wife and children for me!

At that point Shirley invited me back to play in the band in Cheyenne. While I was there, the married piano player she was going to fire, kissed me. After she decided to fire the guitar player instead and have two piano players, I had the choice to stay if I wanted to, but I decided to play for a week, take the money and go to England, to see my Auntie Agnes (Granddad's sister) one more time before she died.

Looking For My Roots: England

I became close friends with the manager of a motel lounge in my home town after I worked there as a cocktail waitress. I arranged to meet her in London, and we talked about moving to Nashville where she would be my manager and I would be her artist.

But in England I had an epiphany. At a party I realized all of a sudden that I didn't want to be a part of all that anymore. I didn't know what it was I wanted, but I knew it was not that. So I left and got on a train to Birmingham, to see Uncle Harry, my grandmother's brother.

Nana had told me about her brother, Harry. He was a singer and a musician. He had made his living on the stage. At last, I got to meet him in person. He lived by himself in the city of Birmingham with his solitary dinners and his flower garden. His dear wife had passed on.

His smile radiated joy. His blue eyes sparkled with inner light. His voice soothed my soul. But then I was born to hear that accent. I would have heard it first in my mother's womb. I was told I even had an English accent before I was five. I had been raised hearing my grandparents' English accents, drinking tea, and eating Welsh cakes. So when I was in England it was like going home.

After visiting my great-uncle, I took the train to Southampton to see my Auntie Agnes. I soon discovered my maternal grandfather's sister was a spiritualist, that is, she communed with the dead. I attended a séance with her and her group once. We sat around in a circle and someone supposedly conjured up dead people. One of the women supposedly contacted my grandfather. She said a bunch of stuff about how people had let me down.

I didn't get much out of the psychic reading, but Auntie Agnes was a link to my grandfather who died in 1971, and I had not made it home from Mexico to attend his funeral. Seeing her made me feel closer to him.

In England, I enjoyed going to pubs, where I sat around talking and feeling connected to people. We have no counterpart here. Not in bars, not at 12-step meetings, and, unfortunately, not in church. Part of me simply fit into England like a puzzle piece. Still, somehow I had hoped for more. Going to England was what Mom always wanted more than anything else. Maybe part of that desire was just the idea of going back to how things were before they got messed up. Although I was never homesick for Topeka I have often been homesick for the way things used to be.

Jesus Speaks to Mom

Ghosts and paranormal phenomena seem to be even more popular in England than in the United States. My mother was always interested in ghosts and extrasensory perception and astral projection and mixed these ideas in with her beliefs about God. Mom told me many times about a time her soul left her body after an automobile accident. But Mom told me once that Jesus had spoken to her.

"You believe in all these other things," she told me he said to her. *"Why don't you believe in me?"* Sounds like Jesus to me. Mom identified the voice as belonging to Jesus. So do I.

The Power of Music

I identified with songs like "A Whole Lot More of Jesus and a Lot Less Rock 'n' Roll" that Linda Ronstadt had recorded. I can't say that I understood what a "whole lot more of Jesus" meant, but I liked the sound of the music.

Every time I saw Aunt Dot, she told me about how Jesus had died for my sins. One day her eyes filled with tears when she heard me sing with some friends. One of the songs was "Silver Threads and Golden Needles."

"Maybe one day you'll sing your songs for Jesus," she said with tears in her eyes. I had no idea what she was talking about, but that is what happened.

The Search for What is Still Missing

So, in my search for meaning, purpose and love, and to escape the grinding reality of my life, I went looking for fulfillment in art, music and romance. Even when I traveled to England, I was doing what many refer to as "looking for my roots." I found them. But something was still missing.

People are always searching for what is missing in their life, that something we can't quite put our finger on, what we still reach for when we think we've found it. While you pursue loves that do not really satisfy, Christ still holds out his offer of what it is you and I are really looking for; he knows because he made us. Find God and all your other loves can become properly aligned.

St. Augustine said, "Thou hast prompted him, that he should delight to praise thee, for thou hast made us for thyself and restless is our heart until it comes to rest in thee."

Essential # 16 for finding your sweet spot: Love God

Putting God first made all the difference. That's when I stepped into his plan for my life. Before, I didn't understand that I was created to love and be loved by God. If we place other loves first in our hearts there will always be problems, but once we know him in a personal way, other things will begin to fall into place. Not in the sense that everything suddenly starts to go your way, but when you know God, you know you can trust him. I did not know this truth during all those years of searching but I know it now. The love of God is the love we are meant to experience, the "something missing" in our lives. Without him we can never fulfill the purpose for which we were born.

Holy Spirit, I am thankful that you worked in my heart to draw me to you and I ask you now to keep your hand firmly around me and keep me near. Please keep revealing yourself to me and how my life can reflect who you are to those around me.
In Jesus' name. Amen.

CHAPTER 17

SEEING JESUS – TRANSFORMATION

Transform: 1. To change markedly the *form* or appearance of. 2. To change the nature, function or condition of; convert.

> *Therefore, if anyone is in Christ, he is a new creation; old things have passed away; behold, all things have become new (2 Corinthians 5:17).*

My life was already half over before I really began to live. I started to live when I quit running from God in 1979. I was thirty-three.

After leaving Nashville and going to England, I returned to Topeka with an incomprehensible urge to go to California. I felt like the ocean was calling me. My friend Rita from Topeka got me a job at a motel lounge in Costa Mesa, and I was off in my white 1971 Ford Econoline van with the orange carpet – the one the butterfly died in.

I went to Costa Mesa, California, in 1979 to play at that lounge. My name was on the marquee. Wow! It was a new day.

I played mostly country ballads on a piano and sang in the lounge of the motel from 5:00 to 9:00 p.m. five or six nights a week. From 9:00 to 1:00 a guy with the initials J.C. played old rock 'n' roll songs and talked between songs. At the end of the night he played strange songs. One of the songs was "Open My Eyes, Lord." I thought that was kind of weird, but I liked it and went to my room and tried to play it. It turned out to be harder than it sounded, but I faked it and sang it some in my room.

He played another song that went like this: "Hear my cry, Oh, God, attend unto my prayer. From the ends of the earth, shall I cry unto you, and when my heart is overwhelmed, lead me to the Rock that is higher than I, that is higher than I" (Psalm 62:1-2). I had never heard songs like this.

He also sang these words: "I will sing unto the Lord as long as I live, I will sing praise to my God while I have my being. My meditation of Him shall be sweet, I will be glad, I will be glad in the Lord. Bless thou the Lord, Oh, my soul, praise ye the Lord, bless thou the Lord, Oh, my soul, praise ye the Lord" (Psalm 104:33 KJV).

The guy seemed kind of religious, but he was nice. I talked to him one time after he played a set. In the course of our conversation, he asked me if I had ever talked to Jesus about my soul. He said it in a non-threatening way, kind of just asking.

A bunch of people, including patrons of the lounge and cocktail waitresses, sang those strange songs with him at the end of the night. Sometimes after listening to him for a while I went up to my room and dug out the Gideon's Bible and tried to read it. I didn't understand it much, but there was something about hearing this guy's music that made me want to start reading the Bible.

One day at the swimming pool I met some people from Germany and France and Belgium. David was English. His wife, Gisela, was German, and they lived in Belgium. The other guy was French. I could speak a little French so we talked a little bit. But all he could do was talk about Jesus non-stop, about all the things he used to do that Jesus delivered him from.

I was reading a book by J. Krishnamurti at the time. He was an Indian who spoke all over the world. At the time, I found it enlightening, thought provoking and it kept my interest. But this David talked to me about how Jesus had *changed his life*. That was an interesting concept that I hadn't thought much about. Changed his life; I wondered how, what that might mean.

I had been approached by Jehovah's Witnesses, Mormons and

Moonies (followers of Sun Yung Moon). I had stopped short of going to a Transcendental Meditation meeting when they said I had to bring a flower and a piece of fruit. Not my type of deal. I had looked into Baha'i, thought about Wicca in college and later got into *I Ching* and Astrology, tried the Ouija Board and started reading the *Urantia Book*. All these things supposedly brought you into contact with "the divine" or the Tao or the future or something.

I was very interested in all this. However, these different approaches to spirituality merely skated across the surface of my curiosity without taking hold. Nothing in my life really changed; I just had these intriguing ways of thinking and talking about them. Actually, they just gave me a false sense of control that I really didn't have.

I even had a strange spiritual experience after smoking marijuana and reading the *Urantia Book*, in which I felt like a burning piece of tumbleweed spinning across a field in the Kansas plains. This was trippy but it didn't make my life any better.

I really was not too interested in this guy taking me away from my book, but he was so nice. They all were. They were nice to be around. They had something attractive about them. I wanted to be near them even though they seemed to be preoccupied with talking to me about Jesus. They obviously didn't understand that I had already done that bit about asking Jesus to be my Lord and Savior.

Besides wanting to be around them I also wanted to do something nice for them. So when they said they planned to take a bus to church I offered to take them. They all piled into my van and off we went to a large auditorium in Anaheim.

When we got to the meeting the sermon was over. What may have happened is that we thought it started at 7:30 when it actually started at 7:00. Hal Lindsay had spoken and now he was in front of the church where people could talk to him.

The English David went with me up front and described me to Hal Lindsay as a "backslidden gospel singer." Actually, I was neither, but it didn't matter. God knew. Lindsay prayed for me. He asked God to lead me and fulfill his will in my life, which he is still doing.

A few minutes later my new friends asked me if they could pray with me. At first I was reluctant, but then agreed. They all joined hands around me in a circle. Some were praying in tongues; it sounded like a mountain stream. I don't remember any words, but I remember crying. I remember it like it was yesterday. The date was July 15, 1979, the day I finally gave my life to Jesus. Before this, the only thing I really remembered like yesterday was the first time I heard the word "divorce."

That night in Anaheim, I saw a vision of Jesus superimposed on the auditorium floor, walking across the sand, wearing a white robe and sandals. I felt his presence in a way I had not felt it before – a sense of his nearness – like liquid love being poured all over me. I think I even smelled a fragrance something like roses. Then, "Heaven came down and glory filled my soul." Life has never been the same since. Jesus said, "He who has My commandments and keeps them, it is he who loves Me. And he who loves Me will be loved by my Father, and I will love him and manifest Myself to him" (John 14:21).

The next day I got fired from my job at the motel lounge without any explanation. The boss just told me it was over. So there I was stuck out in California without a job. Kind of reminded me of the time in New York State when I ended up on the street. But the outcome was a lot different. This time I had been found by God.

A waitress at the lounge had mentioned Calvary Chapel. I thought I would check it out. So I went there the following Sunday morning. I met Pastor Chuck Smith and he gave me the name of a Christian singer-songwriter who had a big hit in Christian music at the time, which later became a standard in Christian music. I ended up staying at her house with her roommate until she came back from a mission trip. I even think it was six days, the same number of days I was in jail in Mexico. Again, a whole lot different this time. Last time God freed me but I still had not been found.

Her roommate told me she was "as big as the Beatles" in Christian music. I was beginning to understand that there was a difference between being "in the world" and being "in the Lord."

After about six days at their house, the church made arrangements for me to stay at this place called "The Lord's House."

My first morning waking up at "the Lord's House" in Costa Mesa in 1979, a clear, kind, audible male voice said to me, *"If you were looking at an orange tree, would you expect an apple to fall out?"* I didn't know what the words meant, but the sound of the voice was incredible.

I have pondered all these years what those words meant. Sometimes it's as simple as "You are unique. Don't try to be like anyone else." More specifically, "You are altogether a different species than you were, as different as apples and oranges." Jesus referred to bad trees that cannot bear good fruit and vice versa, another illustration of transformation that occurs once we believe God's forgiveness is for us personally.

"Therefore, if anyone is in Christ, he is a new creation; old things have passed away; behold, all things have become new," Paul wrote to the church in Corinth. "Now all things are of God, who has reconciled us to Himself through Jesus Christ, and has given us the ministry of reconciliation, that is, that God was in Christ reconciling the world to Himself, not imputing their trespasses to them, and has committed to us the word of reconciliation.

"Now then, we are ambassadors for Christ, as though God were pleading through us; we implore you on Christ's behalf, be reconciled to God. For He made Him who knew no sin to be sin for us, that we might become the righteousness of God in Him" (2 Corinthians 5:17-21).

"Now all things are of God..." He is already LORD, but what became real to me is that when Christ saved me and came to live on the inside of me, he became *my* Lord. I had been bought and what I experienced was a down-payment. I realized God made everything and owns everything and that Jesus died for *my* sins. Then I understood that he has a right to take complete control of my life and use it for his purposes.

Essential # 17 on finding your sweet spot: Transformation

You can trust God with all your life. He made you. Trust God to do with you what he desires. Then be transformed by the renewing of your mind by the word of God (Romans 12:1). You will be so grateful that being an ambassador for Christ will be the only possible response.

Father, you gave your Son to die for me. You rose again. Your Spirit lives in me. The least I can do is live for you. Help me stay strong.
In Jesus' name. Amen.

CHAPTER 18

LOUISIANA LESSONS – DISCERNMENT

Discernment: 1. The act or process of discerning. 2. Keenness of discrimination; perspicacity.
Discern: 1. To perceive (something obscure or concealed); detect. 2. To recognize or comprehend mentally.
Discerning. Showing insight and judgment; perceptive.
Perspicacity: Acuteness of perception, discernment or understanding.

*... and after the fire a still small voice (*I Kings 19:12).

In the "Jesus of Nazareth" film I watched where, after casting the demons out of the Gadarene demoniac, Jesus tells him to go back and tell the people in the town what had happened to him. I felt God was telling me through this film to return home and let people know what had happened to me. So, after staying four months in "The Lord's House" in Costa Mesa, I went to Topeka. To my utter disbelief, nobody was thrilled. I still haven't figured that out. I had found God. I had found life. I had found what I had been looking for all my life. And all they did was act like I was weird.

After a couple of months in Topeka, I decided to call some of my Nashville friends and see if I could go play some music. I ended up going to Milwaukee, Wisconsin, to play with a friend I had met in

Nashville. Her lead guitar player was a self-confessed "backslidden Christian."

While in Milwaukee a bartender developed a crush on me. I talked to him about Jesus and some girl practically got in a fight with me. "Why are you working here and talking to people about religion?" she said. I didn't really know. But we were only there a week. So it didn't matter very much. One time when I was in the world some girl had wanted to pick a fight with me because she thought I was talking to our guitar player who was her boyfriend. This woman wanted to fight about me talking about Jesus. I guess some people just want to fight about anything.

Traveling back from Milwaukee I ran into freezing rain, and before I knew it the van was slipping. From eyewitness reports my van turned all the way over before landing right side up in a ditch. An angel must have been holding me steady while the van turned over around me. The windshield had popped out. All I remember is that I called a pastor of a church who came and got me and took me to his house where I stayed until my van was ready to drive back to Topeka. It was during the Christmas season.

Back in Topeka I got a job working in the office of a furniture and appliance sales and service center that was downtown at the time. Not quite what I had in mind.

In 1979 I thought in about six months I would be in an evangelistic ministry, playing in a band, telling people about Jesus and traveling around. While I was thinking about that, the friend who had gotten me the job in Costa Mesa called and said I should meet her ex-husband. He had had that same Jesus thing that happened to me happen to him.

Joe Barry

Joe Barry had recorded the hit single "I'm a Fool to Care" in 1961. He sounded a lot like Fats Domino, who had also recorded it, but he was white. He had been married to the friend who got me the job in Costa Mesa, where I heard J. C. singing and talking about Jesus, where I met David and Gisela who took me to hear Hal Lindsay preach at the location in Anaheim, where I finally gave my life to Christ.

One day when my friend who had been married to him was talking on the phone with him, she gave the phone to me and soon we were talking about Jesus. When I first started talking to him, he had recently become a Christian and was doing a little singing and preaching in churches. I talked to Joe Barry a handful of times on the phone before moving to Galliano, Louisiana.

He told me he had been on the 700 Club and even had a counseling ministry through that program at the time. The ministry was called "Lion of Judah Ministries." But he wasn't going to church anywhere currently. He told me he loved the Lord but had problems with some of the Lord's people.

We had talked on the phone a few times and I felt like we were buddies, true kindred spirits. He had a warm, soothing voice. It was deep, rich and hoarse, and he had that Cajun accent. He said he had met a number of celebrities, including Elvis Presley, B.J. Thomas and Cher during his glory days in the music business.

He said he had become a millionaire after his first hit record. Then he lost it, spent it on drugs and booze and women. But after he lost his money, he turned to the Lord. He married again and got divorced again. When I knew him he was divorced. I called him up one night discouraged about something.

'You Sound Like You've Lost Your Joy'

"You sound like you've lost your joy," he told me one day on the phone. "You ought to come down here and meet some of the people in the church down here."

Living on the bayou in Louisiana turned out to be one of the best times of my life. Long story short, I moved in with him and his mother and stayed for about six weeks (not in his room or in his bed). At the time, I thought I would be going on the road for Jesus.

Every time I saw him he had what seemed like hundreds of prescription bottles sitting on a dresser nearby. He coughed a lot, and his lungs often sounded completely full of phlegm.

Eventually, he went back to playing secular music in bars, he told me later, after I had moved back to Kansas. On one of those occasions he told me he got shot in the hand. And he told me he had gotten married again, for the third time.

"I have to have somebody to take care of me," he said. I never saw him again, never met his new wife. A few years ago I found out that he had died. I miss him. But I'll see you again, Joe Barry. And the next time I see you, you won't be coughing with a string of pill bottles sitting around.

Contagious Cajun Joy

When I moved out of Joe Barry's house, a family took me in. I had met their son at church. They treated me like a member of their own family. Joe Barry had said to me that I should come down and live among the Cajuns, that they would show me something I needed to see. And they did. I saw their unconditional love, I experienced their generosity, and I soaked up their contagious joy.

I slowed down for a while in Louisiana. There was something about living on the bayou. The first time I saw one of those drawbridges and saw those shrimp boats floating down the bayou I thought I had gone back in time a hundred years.

I loved the way the Cajuns talked, I loved to hear the old relatives speak French, and I loved drinking Community Coffee. Most of all I just enjoyed their love. There seemed to be no limit to it. And I soaked that up too.

Because of Jesus, we all had a lot in common, and our souls were comfortable together. Jesus makes this possible. Living on Bayou Lafourche in South Louisiana, I experienced crawfish boils, learned how to make roux and gumbo and jambalaya, and, more than that, I learned what it was to be taken into the family of God.

"Nobody's ever done this for you, have they?" said the mom of the family who took me in. It's true I had never been taken in like that. There is a verse in the Bible about it and they really lived it. "God sets the solitary in families," it says in Psalm 68:6. Next I moved in with a woman in Golden Meadow I met in the singles group at church. I worked at a pizza restaurant for a time, at a fast-food hamburger restaurant in Galliano for three months, and for a short time in a Christian bookstore on Bayou Lafourche whose owner was a lady from Panama. Her name was Luz – light.

Full Gospel Tabernacle in Cut Off

For a while, I lived in a tiny trailer behind the Full Gospel Tabernacle in Cut Off. I met my second husband through an evangelist that came to preach somewhere in the neighborhood. It had been six years since I had divorced my first husband. I thought it was kind of interesting that six years was also the approximate amount of time between my mother's divorce from my dad and her marriage to my stepfather.

I did not listen to my friends who were telling me I was being hasty. My future husband and I had only known each other five weeks. I was praying for God's will, but my emotions were speaking a lot louder than my spirit at that time. I could not hear God's voice over my loneliness. I thought a person could heal my loneliness. After the breakup of my second marriage, I decided to go back home to Kansas.

Imprisoned By Loneliness

Before leaving South Louisiana I had accompanied a couple of women from church to visit their boyfriends who were incarcerated.

I had had a lot of fun at those church services. The guys seemed to do a lot of art or played music and some of them read the Bible and many of them had found Christ. It was actually quite an inspiration to be in church with them, because they seemed so dedicated to the

Lord. I was impressed by the fact that these guys didn't have a whole lot of distractions and therefore could easily devote themselves to Bible study and prayer. They certainly knew that they needed the Lord, and they seemed to appreciate that the life they were living now, even though behind bars, was a drastic improvement over the life they were living before they met Christ.

I moved back to Kansas after my second husband left. Then as soon as the divorce was final I started getting collect calls from someone in Louisiana. He wrote me every day. I didn't care that my phone bills were sky high.

He said he had seen my picture in my friend's wallet when she came to visit her boyfriend. I don't really know why, but as soon as I started talking to him it didn't take long before I was emotionally involved with this person. You guessed it. That was my addiction: Falling in love with love.

'At Least I Know Where He is Every Night'

"Well, this is cool. At least I know where he is every night," I remember thinking when I first started talking to him.

"Where will he go when he gets out if he doesn't marry me?" I also remember thinking, as if this were my responsibility.

The first night he called collect, I did not accept. But I felt so guilty that the second time he called I accepted. It didn't take long for me to get hooked. Getting hooked by people in need can be dangerous.

For one thing, I was on the rebound from marriage number two, I was ready to be wanted and needed again, and my new love interest seemed to want and need me. Satan knows our weaknesses.

Before the Calls Started

Before the calls started, I had been living in a trailer with a woman who went to my church. I was working at an institute for children and adults with developmental disabilities, as an activity therapy aide. I kept my keys in the pocket of my jeans and tried to find stimulating activities for profoundly developmentally disabled children and adults, ranging in age from six to twenty-one.

I learned how to play Yahtzee with people with severe disabilities. They enjoyed the sound of the dice in the cup and as they fell onto the table. Someone explained to me that, although their bodies had developed normally, these people had the cognitive abilities of infants. But one thing I learned. They were people, individuals with emotions and the capacity to receive love, sometimes even give it, however limited.

Louisiana Take Two

At first he wanted to marry me without my even going to Louisiana. This can actually be done. Thankfully, someone compelled me to meet him in person before marrying him. I decided to move to Louisiana and visit him as often as I could. So that's what I did.

He had connections with a halfway house ministry in Baton Rouge. He told them about me and I went to stay there. People went to this facility when they got out of prison. Only women stayed there at the time.

When I got to Louisiana, I started looking for a job. I got a job as a secretary for half a day and as a preschool teaching assistant for another half day.

Then I met my future roommate, a physical education major from Louisiana State University, who was running a recreation center in Baton Rouge. She said she was looking for a Christian to work in the playschool. I became her employee, her friend, and, finally, her roommate. We moved into a house together and she became almost my constant companion for the next six years.

The Complete Friend

She was a few inches taller and stockier than I and had dark hair, dark eyes and a pretty face. She was Italian, born and raised in Kenner, a suburb of New Orleans, and she said that by her accent, a lot of people thought she was from New York.

Her voice naturally modulated. She could have worked on the radio. My first husband has a voice like that too. He can turn his radio voice on and off. Only she never turned hers off. Her voice sounded like the radio all the time.

She said the first time she saw me I looked thin and undernourished. From then on she called me "Bones." So she made sure I had something healthy to eat every day. We had steamed broccoli and carrots every night at the center, cooked on a hot plate. After I met her I ate plenty of that. She also cooked lots of pasta with spaghetti sauce.

She had a charismatic personality that I was instantly drawn to. For a long time, we enjoyed doing things together more than doing them with anyone else. We always had fun together. I enjoyed being near her. She made me laugh.

She came with me to meet my inmate boyfriend one time and wasted no time telling me she did not trust him. She said our relationship was not healthy. But I proceeded to pursue marriage with my boyfriend.

We had planned to get married. I had already bought rings in Topeka. I had a letter of permission from the warden and I had a license. We were going to get married before he got out.

How God Prevented a Wedding

The day the wedding was planned it rained so hard in Baton Rouge there was no way I could drive. The night before, I had no peace either. I couldn't figure out why I wasn't happy about getting married the next day. I woke up and I thought God had changed His mind about flooding the world again.

Don't Let the Devil Steal Your Song!

Since the torrential downpour had prevented me from driving some distance in blinding rain, I decided to go later that afternoon and try to smooth things over. Upon my arrival, I got checked in and waited for him to join me at a table. I remember after he sat down he told me we were both going to say our piece and then we were not going to see each other again. Instead we made up and decided to see if we could still get married. By the time we made that decision the warden had gone home for the day.

Throughout this relationship, God spoke to me twice.

"It's time to get out," the still, small voice said (pretty loud on the inside, actually), the first time.

"Extricate," he said, the second time. This was a word I had to look up in the dictionary. Next, after the torrential downpour that should have kept me at home, God made sure the warden was gone when we were about to destroy our lives. And, finally, the boyfriend said God told him not to marry while he was incarcerated.

The 'Complete Friend'

My roommate and I moved north to get our master's degrees. Later we would move together to another state to get our Ph. D.'s.

I got a master's degree in family relations and child development. I believe now I thought that way I might figure out the chaos in my own family. I wanted to know all about what divorce and dysfunction did to families. I wanted to become a marriage and family counselor so I could help others. I know, you're thinking, *really?*

I felt like my roommate was all I needed in a friend. I had not been closer emotionally to anyone than I became with her. I really felt I didn't need any other friends. It was kind of a complete relationship. It worked for both of us for a long time until she found a new friend. And eventually, she moved away. I will always be grateful to her for being a second pair of eyes to see what was wrong with my relationship with my friend in prison and I do miss her.

How God Speaks

During all this time, I learned a lot about the voice of God. He speaks through his Word, the Bible, through people, in our hearts, and in our circumstances. He sets things up to prevent us from destroying our lives as he did when he prevented me from marrying into a situation that may have been disastrous. If our deepest desire is to be a follower of Jesus and be his disciple, God is very interested in us learning how to communicate with him. He has proven himself over and over again in this regard.

Essential # 18 for finding your sweet spot: Discernment

God will speak to you if you are willing to listen. He will guide you into all truth and protect you. Be careful what spirit you listen to and don't ignore a lack of peace about something. It could save your life.

Father, thank you for keeping me from getting into a whole lot more trouble than I did, and please help me be more sensitive to your voice.
In Jesus' name. Amen.

CHAPTER 19

MOVING ON – HOPE

Hope. 1. To wish for something with expectation of its fulfillment.

Jesus said to her, "I am the resurrection and the life. He who believes in Me, though he may die, he shall live. And whoever lives and believes in Me shall never die. Do you believe this?" (John 11:25, 26)

But I don't want you to be ignorant, brethren, concerning those who have fallen asleep, lest you sorrow as others who have no hope (1 Thessalonians 4:13).

Perhaps because of the proliferation and wide acceptance of divorce today, people are writing new books about "blended families." I recently saw one telling children that divorce is "not the end of the world." Well, it may not be the end of *their* world, but it sure can be the end of a *child's* world. Still, although there really are no "good" divorces, ours could have been a lot worse.

Though we missed out on living with him, and were guests in his home, we relied on the regularity of our three visits a week with Dad. And, years later, when I spent time with Dad and Peggy, God put a piece back into my heart.

"*I am sorry* I could not provide that security for you," Dad said to me once, referring to the security his parents provided for him by staying together. Amazing what three little words can do.

Saved at Sixteen at a Baptist Revival

I came to know Jesus Christ July 15, 1979, in Anaheim, California. But I had never heard anyone in my immediate family talk about that experience until 1992, when my father came to Stillwater, Oklahoma, to see me receive my master's degree. For some reason I started singing "Love Lifted Me" and my dad started singing along. "Where did you learn that song?" I said.

"I was saved at a Baptist revival when I was sixteen," he told me. I was surprised because at the time he was living with his girlfriend between his third and fourth wives and I had reproached him about it.

"I don't need to hear that," he had said to me. It was one of the few times I had seen him upset with me.

When I was little we attended Grace Cathedral in Topeka, probably because it was close to the Church of England, where Mom came from. He went to church off and on throughout his life; seems like it depended on if his wife went or not. With Mom, he did, with Irene, he did not, with the third wife, yes, with the fourth wife, yes, with the girlfriend, no. And, finally, in the end, he completely lost interest.

"Do you think much about Jesus?" I asked him one day.

"No, I don't think too much about that," he said. "I've got too many other things to think about." Sometimes he would talk like that; other times he would agree with me that God and Jesus and the Bible were important. The disease seemed to weave in and out like that, between years, between thought structures.

Salvation is Forever

Even though Dad told me he had been saved at a Baptist revival when he was sixteen, sometimes he seemed to have forgotten. Once

I told him I had gone to a tent revival the night before and he rolled his eyes. Another time, I asked him if he knew the Lord and he said he knew "of" him.

I had lost him to divorce and dementia and I would soon lose him to death. I desperately did not want to lose him for eternity. I hoped Jesus had included my dad when he said *no one would snatch those that were his out of his hand* (John 10:28). Anyway, only God knows the true condition of a heart.

'Drunk with the Wine of the World'

When David came to see Dad after he had entered the nursing home, he commented on the juxtaposition of jubilation over the inauguration of America's first black president with the horrors of "putting our parents away" when they age.

At significant times in our history, apparently our society approves of including clergy in the celebration of certain events, in this case honoring the rich Christian experience of the African-American community. I was particularly struck by the eloquence of these words.

The Reverend Joseph Lowery, octogenarian who gave the benediction after the inauguration of Barack Obama, January 20, 2009, said, "(Guide us) ... lest we, drunk with the wine of the world, forget thee..."

'Going Home to See My Dad'

Dad wanted to go for a long time before he finally died.

"I'm going home to see my dad," he told me one day in the reception area at the nursing home. Even before his hip replacement, through which he suffered a great deal of pain, he seemed ready to go. After the surgery he declined rapidly.

They were suggesting just giving him medication for the pain because of the risk of the surgery at his age, I suppose. But the amount of medication needed to lessen the pain would have rendered him fairly unresponsive. So we decided on the surgery. It was hard on him.

"I want to go home pretty soon," he told me, before David came for the final visit before the surgery and the hospital stays, in January 2011. I think he meant "going home" in the sense of "going home to be with the Lord." I asked him if he could wait two weeks until after David came.

"That's a long time," he said. But he did wait.

"I'm about to die. I love you," he told David during the month before he died. The rest of what they said is David's story.

February 6, 2011: The Last Time I Saw Him

The last time I saw him I told him I loved him so much and we would be together forever. I was playing a gospel CD that filled me, and I hoped him, with hope. But when he died I could not believe how much I missed him. How could I wait until forever to see him again?

Not having been around when my grandparents died, and therefore having never really gone through the death of anybody before, I had no idea what to expect. No one had told me what to look for. Even though hospice services provided notebooks with information about what to look for when your loved one is dying, I had not been reading them. He had had a stroke and could not speak or swallow. And I had seen the look of death on his face. Still, it hadn't occurred to me that he would die that night.

It's so horrible watching somebody die. Had I expected him to recover? Could I even imagine life without him? I went home that night about 9 p.m., fully expecting to see him again the next day. Instead, I got the call about 1:00 in the morning informing me that he had died. The next time I saw him was at the funeral home. His hands and face were cold and I wept from the soles of my feet.

'Blue-eyed Little Daughter, Sitting on My Knee'

After we buried Dad, David picked up several boxes of books from the house where Dad and Peggy had last lived. I ran across this poem called "Netsie" in one of his books, *The Rhymes of Ironquill*, by Eugene Ware (1939). I could almost hear my father's voice when I read it, and the poem seemed to speak to me from the grave.

> "...Blue-eyed little daughter,
> Sitting on my knee,
> Though I may be buried
> I will grieve with thee."

When grief is fresh, the heart is as tender as a newly dug grave after a spring rain. There is no acceptance of the death of someone so dear. But I believe God will one day wipe every tear from our eyes (Revelation 7:17). Christ's resurrection has taken away the sting of death (1 Corinthians 15:55), and we no longer have to sorrow as others who have no hope (1 Thessalonians 4:13). Jesus is the resurrection and the life, and whoever believes in him will never die (John 11:25). I am glad for the hope of all who have put their trust in Jesus, that he is preparing a place for us with him for eternity (John 14:2). But it still hurts.

> "When the ache is ended,
> We can go and see
> Our old home in Lyra,
> Where the rainbows be..."
>
> Eugene F. Ware, *The Rhymes of Ironquill*

How I long to see him "when the ache is ended." Maybe I will still get to see the house he never got to show me in Pretty Prairie and reminisce about "our old home" in Topeka when we were a family. "Netsie" reminded me of words Dad had spoken to me not long before he died.

'Play it Hard'

When I talked to him on the phone, I heard Daddy's voice the way he sounded on the tapes he made with us when David and I were little, and I felt close to him again. Hearing his voice, still resonant, clear and strong after years of debating, lobbying, adjudicating, speaking, laughing and singing, I was his little girl again.

One afternoon while pedaling the bike at the gym and talking to him on my cell phone, I heard the most amazing words.

"My little daughter," he said to me, "Sometimes in trouble, sometimes in great things. Play it hard."

I didn't always understand him, but this time the message came through loud and clear, even as an insidious disease attacked his beautiful mind.

"Let me know how I can help," he said. "Don't worry, just work on it when you can." I never told him my book focused almost exclusively on him.

Hope of Seeing Him Again

My father deserves praise for all his accomplishments: Serving as probate judge of Shawnee County, Kansas, from 1951-1957; running for lieutenant governor in 1958; and serving as a Navy lieutenant on an LST at Omaha Beach. But for me, one of his greatest accomplishments was reading to me when I was two. And I have the hope of seeing him again because he got saved when he was sixteen.

Essential # 19 for finding your sweet spot: Hope

No matter what has happened or what has been done to us, we all fall short of the glory of God and need his forgiveness. Jesus, God's Son, suffered the punishment for all the sin that would ever be committed. Christ's resurrection gives us hope for our life in this world and after death for all who will.

Don't Let the Devil Steal Your Song!

"… He poured out His soul unto death, and He was numbered with the transgressors, and He bore the sin of many, and made intercession for the transgressors … (Isaiah 53:12)," He prays for us even when we don't know how to pray (Romans 8:26). And when he comes into our heart, our hope is in him. "Christ in you, the hope of glory" (Colossians 1:27).

Father, thank you for your mercy poured out on us and for making intercession for us. It gives me hope that you came, you lived, died, and rose again and sent the Holy Spirit to live in us so that we can have "strength for today and bright hope for tomorrow." Thank you for giving us your Word and yourself. Thank you for the guidance of your Spirit, the peace, the comfort and the hope that living in your presence freely gives to all who will believe in you. Help me remain conscious of this amazing reality.

In Jesus' name. Amen.

Chapter 20

STILL MY HERO – PATIENCE

Patience: The quality of being patient; capacity of calm endurance.

"...Now the parable is this: The seed is the word of God. Those by the wayside are the ones who hear; then the devil comes and takes away the word out of their hearts, lest they should believe and be saved. But the ones on the rock are those who, when they hear, receive the word with joy; and these have no root, who believe for a while and in time of temptation fall away. Now the ones that fell among thorns are those who, when they have heard, go out and are choked with cares, riches, and pleasures of life, and bring no fruit to maturity. But the ones that fell on the good ground are those who, having heard the word with a noble and good heart, keep it and bear fruit with patience" (Luke 8:11-15).

After our parents separated but before Dad married our stepmother, David said he dreamed he was in a huge church with stairs like those in our father's office building at the old First National Bank building at Sixth and Kansas Avenue in Topeka. He was looking down at a couple getting married and he knew who it was.

He said he was trying and trying to run away but all that happened was he would get to another floor and when he looked down the only difference was that the image would be smaller, but he could never get away from it. He said that the dream was prophetic.

With the passage of time, we may have gained some distance from the divorce, but we have never been able to get away from it. As M. Craig Barnes wrote, "The broken heart may eventually heal, but the scars remain." Undeniably, the divorce was the *major event* of our childhood.

David said that with the Alzheimer's we were losing him even though he was still alive. I felt also that we were both losing him and looking for him all our lives. Daddy's "little family" started out with great promise, like Adam and Eve in the Garden of Eden. But just like when sin entered the Garden of Eden and cursed mankind, the divorce cursed our family.

In the Garden of Eden everything started out perfect. Then sin came in. We started out in a perfect environment – safe, secure, intact. The devil tries to destroy all our lives, but God is greater.

My Father Reading to Me

The picture of my father reading to me reminds me of the safety and security the Lord offers to all who will trust him. It is also a picture of a father instructing a child, the way I picture God teaching me every day.

Anyone who reads the Bible with an open heart will discover its power to change lives. The Bible speaks to us about who he is, who we are, how he has revealed himself in history, and how we can come to know him in a way that makes a difference both now and forever.

Jesus compared the Father to natural fathers when he asked if a son asked for bread would any father among them give a stone, or if he asked for a fish, would he be given a serpent? God will not turn anyone away who earnestly seeks the truth about who he is.

Restoration of Something Wrongfully Taken Away

I may have spent more time alone with my dad after he entered the nursing home than I did in my whole life, because David and I had to share him with so many people. When Dad was in the nursing home and I could see him whenever I wanted to, I became aware of a sense of something being restored to me that had been wrongfully taken away. This had happened before when I was able to spend many days with him in Topeka and in Mexico. Now there came yet another level of restoration.

God gave me those opportunities to make up for lost time. He didn't have to do that.

God's love can restore everything. Tragically, most people never discover God's love. This is a very uncomfortable truth.

False Versus Genuine Guilt

I regret not having discovered decades ago that, though my sins were forgiven when I asked Christ into my life, and, though I had forgiven my parents for "ruining my life," I still had psychological and emotional wounds to bring to God for healing.

My parents' divorce was not my fault. I did not ruin their happiness by being born. And I was not responsible for either keeping the divorce from happening or for fixing my family. We may as adults still be carrying around burdens like this and not even know it. There are sins we are guilty for, but false guilt is very destructive. The only sins we are guilty of and need to repent from God will show us if we are willing to find out. And, really, the only sin that keeps us from God is unbelief, because, "Without faith it is impossible to please Him, for he who comes to God must believe that He is, and *that* He is a rewarder of those who diligently seek Him." (Hebrews 11:6).

What Our Parents May Not Have Understood

Our parents probably were not entirely aware that, as their children, we were left standing in the middle between the two people we loved most in the world, picking up the pieces. We made adjustment after adjustment, placed our affections on our father's new mate and family, adjusted to our mother's single life, and would forever be responding to life in ways unalterably affected by their decisions.

Anyone can see that, "All the King's horses and all the King's men cannot put Humpty Dumpty together again." You can't unscramble eggs. We needed to keep on dancing, but we needed some help. Our whole world blew apart in an instant.

Heroes

Heroes are a popular topic for elementary school teachers. As education reporter for the *Johnson County* (Kansas) *Sun*, I attended a school program where fifth-graders celebrated heroes, personal and historical. Female heroes covered a spectrum ranging from Clara Barton to Lucille Ball. The male hero spectrum ranged from Benjamin Franklin to Bill Gates. One little girl chose her sister and another chose her principal. I don't know if any of the 2,000 chose their mother or father as their hero. But there is no question, my Daddy was my hero. He still is. I don't remember a teacher ever asking me who my heroes were but I would have said my dad. I would have said it before the divorce. I would have said it after the divorce. I would still say it today.

"You are my hero," I used to tell him. He just laughed.

My dad was my hero because he sat me between his knees and read to me when I was two. He read *Three Little Kittens* and *The Little Engine That Could*. He was my hero because he came home and talked to my mother, my brother and me about cases involving children in trouble. He made pancakes for us on Sundays. He remembered he used to burp me. I even remember that.

Every morning he drank his coffee and read the newspaper. I took that for granted until he left. For years I missed it until he married Peggy. For most of the eighteen years they were married, until I moved to Topeka in August 2008 and had my own apartment, I enjoyed having breakfast with my Dad while he read the newspaper, even after he began to only read the headlines.

Dad sang and acted in the Kansas Bar shows during the fifties and possibly the sixties, and until he got dementia Dad used to get out his violin and play "Turkey in the Straw." I hope I'll get to hear him play that again someday. But some things are just a gift for now. And even that was one way God had of softening the blow. I believe he's in heaven now and maybe he'll play a violin up there, maybe "Turkey in the Straw," and maybe even "Love Lifted Me."

Being Patient with the Process

The emptiness my daddy's leaving created in my soul was too big to fill with anything but God himself. But even before I came to know Christ, he softened the blow: Trips to Grandpa's farm and Colorado, fishing and horseback riding, homegrown tomatoes, watermelon and homemade ice cream, "squirrel tails," and cherry pie, family reunions, Christmases at Grandpa and Grandma's, piano lessons (and tuna sandwiches and Grapette) at Mrs. Durein's, my friend Gary, the trip to Mexico.

Sometimes we ask why God lets bad things happen in the first place. Well, maybe that's what we need to realize that we need him. But even though we did not know him and were not serving him, God poured out blessings on us and softened the blow of the pain we felt.

Now he is the anchor of my soul. My prayer is that you have seen something in my story that will motivate you to invite Christ into your life if you have not already done so, and if you have, tell someone how Christ changed your life for the better.

And be patient with yourself and with the process. If you feel God is leading you to write your story down, please follow his lead.

If you don't write it down nobody may ever know about it but you. Your story may help somebody. Once you get started God will give you more ideas and help you develop it. You may not think you're a great writer, but your story is your story and nobody can tell it better than you.

Essential # 20 for finding your sweet spot: Patience

You will never have a better friend and comforter than the Lord. He will do miracles in your life every day if you will just turn to him and give him what is rightfully his – your life. He is patient with us. He waits for us to see how all our other gods fail us. He does not force us. And then he wants us to be patient in our dealings with him and with others – and with ourselves.

Father,
You have done so much to prove your love for me and yet I still fall very short. But your Word is filled with encouragement, and your daily presence in my life becomes more real day by day. Thank you, Jesus, for the cross, for the Holy Spirit and for your Word. Help me live a life that honors you and gives you glory.
In Jesus' name. Amen.

Appendix

THE RECORDINGS (1953-1958)

Sometimes Dad's voice sounded so young it reminded me of those tapes he made of us kids as children. "When did that stop?" he asked me. I could not say.

"Good question," I said.

I have preserved the recordings my father made of my brother and me as children, singing and play-acting with him as a radio announcer. He recorded my brother and me in 1953 and later with my stepmother, stepbrother and stepsister.

'The Democrats' Eleventh-Hour Tactic'

The recorded election returns testify that my dad and the incumbent lieutenant governor of Kansas in 1958 ran a close race, but the Democrats defeated them. Unusual for mostly Republican Kansas, George Docking won his second term as governor that year.

During his campaign for lieutenant governor, the Democrats accused my father of unlawfully accepting more than $2,000 in attorney fees while serving as probate judge, related to "sanity hearings" for out-of-county mental patients. He said the routine practice was not illegal, he would abide by any court decision regarding it, and he was not surprised by the Democrats' "eleventh-hour tactic." The other recordings are more light-hearted.

'My Client Cannot Possibly Have Stolen Those Chickens'

1953: After my brother and I take turns singing "How Much is That Doggie in the Window?" a mock court case ensues.
Thump, thump, thump goes the gavel.
"The court will now come to order," he says. "The first case on today's docket is the state of Kansas vs. David Cogswell. The defendant is charged with stealing chickens. How do you plead, guilty or not guilty?"
"Not guilty," says David.
I was cast as his lawyer. There is the sound of rustling paper.
"So, now, you see, your honor, my client cannot possibly have stolen those chickens."
"Very well, you've made a good case. The court has listened to the evidence carefully and has considered it and finds that the defendant is not guilty and should be discharged."
"Say, David, who was that lady I saw you with last night?
"That wasn't a lady. That was my wife."
"Say, Carolyn, have you taken a bath lately?"
"No, Daddy, is there one missing?"
Then we had a man-on-the-street interview session regarding the city elections:
"You told me you were going to vote for Wilkie the other day," my dad said to me. "Do you remember why?"
"Because he's the handsomest."
"Do you still think so?"
"Both of them, their faces are just as handsome as each other," I said.

'COGS Radio, The Crazy Station in the Middle of the Nation'

1957: Dad speaking: "This is COGS Radio, the crazy station in the middle of the nation. Before you hear our program you'll have to listen to a message from our sponsors, the makers of Piggo Perfume." He said I wrote this one.

"Girls, when you go to a party do you want to smell? Just put some Piggo Perfume on the bottom of your feet and when you walk into the room all the boys will go-o-o, "Whew!" Get some at your nearest packing house today."

Singing Together

Dad also recorded us singing together. Much of the recordings were made after the divorce. We all sang old songs together, and my Dad taught me to sing the harmony part to "Tell Me Why," a song popular in the 1940s about the stars shining and about loving someone because God made them. My stepmother, Irene, sang well also. We had a medley of old songs that included "The Old Gray Mare," "In the Evening by the Moonlight" and "Wait Till the Sun Shines, Nellie." It was heaven on earth singing with Dad and Irene.

Dad's Eulogy

I am privileged to call this man Daddy.

How do I find the words to offer a fitting tribute to this man God gave me to be my father, except to say, "I am privileged to call this man Daddy."

Whose knees encased me as he read to me *The Five Little Kittens That Lost Their Mittens* [It was actually *Three Little Kittens*].

Whose strong shoulder I burped on as he patted my little back with his gentle hand.

A hand that gripped the hand of President Eisenhower, Vice-president Nixon, William Allen White, Arthur Capper, Alf Landon, Bob Dole and, undoubtedly many of you here, in a heartfelt and congenial greeting.

His smile lit up a room, his hug drew me to the heart of God, and he always made me feel like I was Daddy's little girl. He even sang it to me:

"You're the Spirit of Christmas, my star on the tree;

You're the Easter Bunny to Mommy and me.

You're sugar and spice and everything nice,

And you're Daddy's Little Girl."

He taught me to sing harmony to a song called "Tell Me Why."

"Tell me why the stars do shine

Tell me why the ivy twine,

Tell me why the skies are blue

And I will tell you just why I love you.

Because God made the stars to shine
Because God made the ivy twine
Because God made the skies so blue
Because God made you, that's why I love you."

In 1992 Dad came to Oklahoma to share an accomplishment with me. All of a sudden, he began to sing, "Love lifted me, love lifted me, when nothing else could help, love lifted me (2x) ..." (and he probably added, "Bom-bom-bom-bom")

"Daddy," I said, "Where did you learn that song?"

"I was saved at a Baptist revival when I was sixteen," he said, and I was glad.

Lately there were times I was afraid he had forgotten and even though I knew God had not forgotten, I was glad when, this past Christmas Eve, I heard him say "Jesus" and bow his head.

So, until I see him again ...

How do I live a life that offers a fitting tribute to this man God gave me to be my father, except to say, "I am privileged to call this man Daddy."

Devotion: The Resurrection and the Life

"I am the resurrection, and the life: He who believes in Me, though he may die, he shall live" (John 11:25).

A month to the day since we buried my father, a large bouquet of roses, carnations, lilies, orchids and sprays of leaves remained atop my piano in the living room. One by one I had removed them as they dried out and began to droop.

For weeks the flowers' fragrance had filled my apartment, and, to the strains of Grieg's "Morning," from "Peer Gynt," I had thought about my father's life and what he meant to me. I had missed him, I had wept and I had inquired of God, "Where is he, Lord?" I asked. "What is he doing? Is he thinking of me? Is he aware of the affairs of this life?" My father's brilliant mind had declined in the later years of his life, but he said he had been saved as a young man.

Near the end of his life he had quit going to church and had been ambivalent in his answers to my questions about his relationship with God. I was worried. But on Christmas Eve I had asked my pastor and his wife to lead him in the sinner's prayer in the recliner in his room at the nursing home.

"Glenn," my pastor's wife said, "Jesus wants to be your friend," as though leading a child to the Lord. "If you want to be his friend, repeat after me: 'Jesus.'"

"Jesus," I heard my daddy say, and I saw his head bow down. I was seated behind his left shoulder and could not see his face, but my pastor said tears spilled onto his shoes.

Noticing how clear the sky was, I emptied the remaining dead flowers into the dumpster, felt the sunshine on my back and returned to my apartment.

Who is Jesus?

In the beginning was the Word and the Word was with God and the Word was God (John 1:1).

For by Him all things were created that are in heaven and that are on earth, visible and invisible, whether thrones or dominions, or principalities or powers. All things were created through Him and for Him. And He is before all things, and in Him all things consist (Colossians 1:16,17).

For there is one God and one Mediator between God and man, the Man Christ Jesus, who gave himself a ransom for all...(1 Timothy 2:5).

Numerous Old Testament prophesies point to Jesus. Christ means *messiah,* or the anointed one (as king, priest or saint), for whom the Jews were waiting. Jesus is the living Word of God (John 1:1).

Jesus Christ, born of a virgin (Isaiah 7:14; Luke 1:26, 27, 30, 31) and having never sinned, met God's standard of perfection. God sent Jesus to die for our sin. After three days, he rose from the dead and was seen by many witnesses

Leaving this world without Christ is too deadly a wager to make. Please don't turn him away!

Jesus said, "I am the way, the truth, and the life. No one come to the Father except through me (John 14:6).

SALVATION PRAYER

"Most assuredly, I say to you, unless one is born again, he cannot see the kingdom of God" (John 3:3).

Jesus said, *"For God so loved the world that He gave His only begotten Son, that whoever believes in Him should not perish but have everlasting life. For God did not send His Son into the world to condemn the world, but that the world through Him might be saved.*

"He who believes in Him is not condemned; but he who does not believe is condemned already, because he has not believed in the name of the only begotten Son of God. And this is the condemnation, that the light has come into the world, and men loved darkness rather than light, because their deeds were evil" (John 3:16-19).

"The word is near you, in your mouth and in your heart" (that is, the word of faith which we preach): that if you confess with your mouth the Lord Jesus and believe in your heart that God has raised Him from the dead, you will be saved (Romans 10:9).

Heavenly Father,
I believe that Jesus is Lord, but now I want him to be my Lord. I believe you sent him to die on the cross in payment for my sins and the sins of the whole world. I know I have lived my life apart from you, and I can bear the weight of my sin no longer. I'm asking you to forgive me and be my Savior and Lord now and forever. Help me to live every day for your glory.
In Jesus' name. Amen.

Knowing God is the Ultimate Privilege

Salvation is only the beginning. You will know that you now know God, but you will want to know him better. If you want to know him better and love him and serve him, talk to him and study his Word and do what he tells you to do both in his Word and by his Spirit. You have entered into a spiritual battlefield, and you will need to learn what that means.

A good place to start is to find a church that feeds your spirit with biblical teaching and preaching, praise and worship, and people who welcome you into the family of God. Sometime soon you will want to be baptized and make a public confession of faith. We must never be ashamed of the Lord or else he will be ashamed of us at his coming.

For the wages of sin is death, but the gift of God is eternal life in Christ Jesus our Lord (Romans 6:23).

Father, give me the faith to keep on believing as a child, that, even as the flowers fade and life here on earth slips away, your promise is eternal life for all who believe in you.

'HE SHINES ALL OVER': FROM PRETTY PRAIRIE TO OMAHA BEACH

Dad used to love to tell us his grandmother's name: Eliza Jane O'Leary. Born in 1870, she married my grandfather's father, George Kirkpatrick Cogswell (1867-1949) in 1888, and they arrived in Kansas from Ohio by covered wagon. My grandfather, Carl Clifford (C.C.) Cogswell, her firstborn, was born February 20, 1889, in Pretty Prairie, Kansas. He died May 7, 1975, in Topeka.

Between Carl's birth and that of his younger brother, Guy Kenneth, arrived two sisters, Edna Faye and Elva Grace. Glenn referred to these as Uncle Guy, Aunt Faye and Aunt Grace.

Glenn's mother, born Susie Alma Schisler, was one of nineteen children born to Benjamin and Matilda Horner Schisler. Susie's mother, Matilda, died at age forty-four in 1890 giving birth to a daughter, also named Matilda, who also died. After Matilda's death, family friends Haden and Martha Long of Pretty Prairie took in Susie, who would have been two by then, and, as far as I know, her twin brother, George.

Matilda's death left nine siblings age fifteen and under. All I know about them are their names – from oldest to youngest, Mary (Molly), Sarah (Sadie), Benjamin, Henry, Archie, Jesse, Katie, Susie and George, who may be the ones in the large oval picture I have hanging in my bedroom.

In a cardboard box I found genealogical records my Uncle Ralph obtained in California, stating that Susie was also known as Susie

Long, and that later her foster mother, Martha Long, married a Mr. Evans. She and Dad referred to her both as "Grandma Long" and "Grandma Evans."

Benjamin and Matilda's oldest child, Anna, was twenty-seven when her mother died. Joseph was twenty-six, John, twenty-five, Will, twenty-three, Martin, twenty-two, Edwin, twenty, Lydia Ellen, nineteen, Charles, eighteen, and Ammi, sixteen. Grandma's mother, Matilda, had her first child at eighteen, but I found no more information on what happened to the family structure when she died. Martha and Haden Long are both reportedly buried in Sego Cemetery, west of Pretty Prairie, Kansas. Some records indicate Susie's father, Benjamin, married a Mary Reed after the death of his wife, but I have little information about Susie's relationship with her father after the death of her mother. The record shows that Benjamin lived until 1921, but it is "Mrs. Martha Long" whose name appears on the wedding invitations to Carl and Susie's February 23, 1910, wedding on my grandmother's birthday.

Also, there are several photographs of family members and perhaps others on a trip to Colorado Springs in 1908 with a gentleman identified as "Dad Schisler" in some of them. In some of the photos everyone is riding burros, and the ladies with their full-length skirts are riding sidesaddle.

Glenn Dale Cogswell

Glenn Dale Cogswell was born February 1, 1922, on a farm in Kingman County, Kansas, the youngest of four sons, to Susie Alma Schisler (1888-1988) and Carl Clifford Cogswell (1889-1975). Carl and Susie had four boys: See names and dates in section called "Cogswell Family – Some Important Dates."

Glenn frequently told his children that his mother was "Pennsylvania Dutch" and a "Dunkard." This term referred to the German Baptist Brethren or Church of the Brethren. I assumed this meant the Dunkards believed in baptism by submersion, rather than by sprinkling. In recent years, my dad said his mother was German, though he never said that when we were little, I guess because it was still so close to the war with the Germans.

My grandfather wrote in *Descendents of John Cogswell* that his father was a farmer and a cattle driver. He said he experienced a three-week cattle drive as the youngest driver in the trip – he was fourteen in 1904 – "I have been permitted to see, and be a part of, the development of our country, a development that cannot be duplicated in the future – unless there should be pioneering on another planet," he wrote.

Carl's cousin, the late Helen Cogswell Trostel, wrote that Carl was a self-taught speaker and writer, not having even a high school education, and that while serving as master of the Kansas State Grange, he was editor in chief of its state publication. Trostel reported that "his proposal to provide an acceptable extension of power to expedite rural electricity at a reasonable rate was presented to the National Grange meeting in Sacramento, California, in 1935 and passed by Congress in 1936" (*Descendents of John Cogswell,* p. 525). Interestingly, he wrote in his column, "Carl's Cogs," against the federal government's plan "to nationalize our school system."

From One-Room Schoolhouse to Topeka High

Glenn, as his three older brothers, attended a one-room rural schoolhouse. Zula Bennington (Peggy) Greene, in an article entitled "Help, Not Punishment, Is Goal of Probate Judge," reported in *The Topeka Daily Capital,* Sunday, August 9, 1953, he was "the only pupil in his grade and the teacher put him through both the first and the second grade in one year."

Glenn reported to "Peggy of the Flint Hills" that he grew up on a farm, milking cows, hoeing potatoes and herding cattle. He told Mrs. Green he owed the latter to a "wise old cow pony the family owned." Glenn said it would be more accurate to say the horse rounded up the cattle, nipping them as a dog does, and that he simply "went along to keep the pony company."

Glenn's parents, Carl and Susie, met at a debate tournament.

Apparently having inherited his parents' verbal abilities, Glenn starred on Topeka High School's debate team and in speaking events sponsored by the Young Republicans throughout his high school career.

Although capable of the most serious of academic endeavors, Glenn also demonstrated an appreciation for and the ability to express humor. A clipping in one of Glenn's scrapbooks, apparently printed in the Pretty Prairie newspaper, says, "Glen Coggswell (sic) of Topeka, came in Monday afternoon to pay his father's debt of two cents tax, which Carl failed to remit when he paid his subscription recently. Glen said:

"I wrote to dad and told him I would pay his debt, but that he might leave me short of finance, and that I would expect him to send me a check."

"This relieves us of sending the marshal to Topeka to collect this debt, for which we are all thankful. Glen is visiting with Mrs. A.C. Evans," that is, his Grandma Evans, his mother's foster mother.

Another version of the story may have appeared in the Topeka paper. Many of the clippings are not dated, although most indicate what newspaper they appeared in, whether the *Topeka Daily Capital,* the *Topeka State Journal,* the *Topeka High School World,* or the *Pueblo (Colorado) Star-Journal:*

"Glen Cogswell, Topeka, son of Carl Cogswell, chairman of the state tax commission, called at the office of the newspaper in Pretty Prairie, the old home of the Cogswells, and handed Editor C. W. Claybaugh two cents. "Dad owes you this in tokens," said Glen. "He forgot to send it in renewing his subscription. Yes, I know he's the head of the tax commission and ought not forget about tokens. But he did. Here's the two cents. Don't send the sheriff after him."

Glenn Plays Violin in the Orchestra at Boswell Junior High School

In a photo in his scrapbook, he is holding his violin, which he played from an early age. In a family photo, his mother and all his brothers are sitting on the front porch of a house with different instruments in their laps.

A story in the front page of one of his scrapbooks, called "Boswell 'Girls' Not All That They Seem" carried a photo showing Glenn in the back row on the right. The article appeared sometime between 1934 and 1936 and says:

> Boys will be boys, even though they have to be girls to do it. Fourteen Hi-Y boys from Boswell school proved the fact a few days ago. It seems the Girl Reserves at Boswell were holding a Major Bowes amateur contest. In no uncertain terms they made it clear that the competition was for girls only. When the contest was well under way, fourteen 'gorgeous girls' appeared, their instruments intact, and displayed their charms and musical accomplishments before the judges.
>
> Needless to say, the 'girls' won first prize. Whether it was awarded on the basis of musical merit or for unique taste in clothes has remained something of a mystery. Anyway, the prestige gained by the win served to help the orchestra get a worthwhile 'contract,' namely, a personal appearance at the Y.M.C.A...
>
> At least two fathers recognized flesh and blood behind lip rouge and flowing skirts in the orchestra. Henry Snyder... discovered Henry, Jr., in a lovely blue creation, leading the orchestra. Art Schober... discovered his son Bob hiding under a cute little white hat and a half a pound of lip rouge, back among the wind instruments...
>
> The applause after each number was more than heartening. The personal appearance was not without its educational value for the drummer of the band. Harry Snyder...brought the house down with a prolonged 'roll' on the snares that reverberated through the rafters ...high above the ceiling of the 'Y' gym.

In Glenn's scrapbook there is an envelope containing a photo likely taken sometime in the 1990s with an index card listing names of Boswell Junior High graduates from Glenn's class and a heading: "Boswell Junior High – Dedication." The picture is of a large, white stone with the date "1922" carved on it, the year of Glenn's birth and presumably also that of Boswell Junior High. This picture in his collection demonstrates that Glenn enjoyed being part of history and valued the friendships he made along the way.

A Lot of Basketball

Dad had always enjoyed watching basketball on television. Basketball was in his soul. I didn't know how much until I found the scrapbook brimming with little clippings about basketball games he played as a youth.

As I touch the yellowed clippings, immaculately pasted on the thick, old pages, I can hear the sound of the balls bouncing on ancient wooden floors and plaster walls, the voices of young boys taunting each other on the court, the sounds of innocence of an age gone by.

Glenn played basketball for Boswell Junior High and for the Indians in the YMCA junior basketball tournaments, in what was referred to as the City League. The other team names were the Midgets, North Topeka and Lafferty's Aces. In the Ripley Park Tourney, he played for the North Topeka Trojans against the Carbondale Oilers.

In 1936, fourteen-year-old Glenn played basketball for his church in the Sunday school league for the Central Congregational Intermediates and the Lowman Methodist seniors. The team standings were "Intermediate," "Senior," and "Adult." The teams played Monday through Thursday at 7 p.m.

In high school, Glenn continued to play basketball in the sophomore intramural basketball league.

"Glenn Cogswell and Kenn Rogers continue to set the pace for the sophomores," the paper reported. "They have 51 and 43 tallies respectively." "Glenn Cogswell is setting the pace with 43 tallies in the three games played."

Glenn clipped an article describing an event featuring Emil S. Liston, a Baker University coach, speaking to men and boys of the Lowman Methodist church. "Recreation as an aid to Christian living will be stressed and recognition will be given to the winning Lowman senior basketball team," the article said. "Seating for the dinner and program will be limited to 400."

Glenn played on the Washburn College basketball squad and played for his fraternity. "Intramural Jottings" columnist Bill Rigby, noted that, "Phi Delts, behind the power of Glenn Cogswell, moved into first place with a victory over Kappa Sigs 21-19. The game ran into overtime, but Cogswell sank a long shot from the side of the court to cinch the game and bring the trophy one step nearer the Phi's." In another column, Rigby stated that Glenn played forward.

Glenn's Early Demonstration of Scholarship, Patriotism, and Debating

At Topeka High School, Glenn was an honor student, a star debater, vice-president of the senior class, and one of four student speakers at his class commencement ceremony.

Glenn followed his parents' example, excelling in debate at Topeka High and advocating for the forensic department (forensics is the art of speechmaking and oral presentation).

During his high school years, Glenn demonstrated a passion for academic excellence and a gift for communication. While a member of the Topeka High School forensics program, Glenn wrote a letter to the high school newspaper advocating for the activity and seeking support for it. He wrote to the editor of the Topeka High newspaper, *The Topeka High World,* that the school was "more widely known for her forensic record than for any other activity.

"In the past six years," he wrote, "Topeka has won the state championship four years successively ... In 1936, Topeka High was awarded the National Sweepstakes, representing the highest average, over a period of five years, of any secondary school in the United States."

"With all due respect to the other activities," he continued, "I believe the forensic department is of more permanent worth, and more worthy of support than any other activity." In the rest of the letter he urged students to support the debaters by offering moral support and by volunteering to act as debate chairmen for the annual debate tournaments held at Topeka High.

In his senior year, 1938-1939, Glenn was an honor student, vice-president of the senior class and one of ten varsity debaters, selected by the debate coach for the National Forensic League. Glenn and Barton Bayly received the degree of distinction from among the four categories of distinction, excellence, merit and honor. The team competed with debaters from Oklahoma, Missouri and Kansas in the Tri-State Debate Tournament in Pittsburg. That year the Topeka team also debated in Kansas City, Salina, Emporia, Lawrence, in Denver, Colorado, and at the Wentworth Military Academy in Lexington, Kansas.

Glenn kept his grades up while participating in a rigorous schedule, traveling every weekend with the debate team. At the Wyandotte debate tournament, Glenn and the Topeka team won second place. The following week, January 20 and 21, in Salina, two of his teammates won first place. According to the *Topeka Daily Capital,* at Emporia, January 27 and 28, 237 debaters on ninety teams from thirty-nine schools participated in a division of the annual College of Emporia (now Emporia State University) invitational debate tournament. At that event, Glenn and his partner did well until they faced the Fort Scott team, bringing home a second place trophy. The following week, Topeka High won first place at the Eastern Kansas conference debate at Topeka High School. Lawrence came in second and Emporia third. The Topeka High *World* reported that the forty-fourth and forty-fifth trophies won by Trojan debaters were shown to the students at a school assembly.

The *Topeka Daily Capital* reported that the Topeka High team was going to Denver to debate the affirmative side of the resolution that "the United States Should Establish an Alliance with Great Britain." According to Edgar Ray Nichols, editor of the *Year Book of College Debating Intercollegiate Debates, 19th edition* (1938), this topic would be the "national High School subject for 1938-1939." On the way, they would stop over in Pueblo to engage in three exhibition debates, two against Centennial High School and one against Central High.

Glenn did not like to lose. *The Pueblo Star-Journal* reported that the Centennial High School team defeated the Topeka team, which was "ranked one of the best teams in the nation." In the photo accompanying the article, seated in the lower left of the photo beside his partner, the winning team beaming behind them, the frown on Glenn's face is palpable, with his eyelids half closed, his eyes rolled upwards and his forehead furrowed. Upon their return from Colorado, the *Topeka High World* explained the Trojan defeat and the consternation on Glenn's face in the photo. Glenn and Harry were "rather dismayed," the high school newspaper reported, to find out they were to debate negatively in Centennial the topic they had prepared to debate affirmatively in Denver. Evidently, no one coached them to prepare both sides of the argument.

After the tournament, The Topeka High School debate coach received two letters of congratulations from speech professors who heard the boys speak. *The Topeka State Journal* reported that the head of the speech department, at the University of Denver, wrote the following in one of the letters:

"They were two of the most effective high school debaters I ever saw. They were, besides, very apparently the finest gentlemen, which isn't always the case with many high school debaters."

Possibly in his junior year, Glenn won first prize in the Shawnee County Young Republican Oratorical contest speaking on the topic "The Constitution Is Essential to Individual Liberties." The first prize was $10. One of his debate partners spoke on, "Must America Fight Another European War?"

Glenn was elected vice-president of the senior class for the following year. That year Glenn and one of his debate team members presented a pro and con argument in the Lowman Methodist Church high school department on the benefits of receiving high school credit for work in the Church School, and presented it to the adult department of the Sunday school Sunday morning!

Glenn was one of four students chosen to deliver the 1939 commencement speech. The theme was "What I Owe America and What America Owes Me." *The Topeka State Journal* reported they based the speeches on the premise that "all men are created equal, with certain inalienable rights, among them life, liberty and the pursuit of happiness." Glenn spoke first. According to the article, in his address, entitled "Our Heritage," he "expounded the glories of an American heritage" and explained that "the sources of liberties enjoyed today have been passed from generation to generation like a torch from runner to runner."

Yearbook Dedications, 1939: 'He Shines All *Over*'

One of Glenn's debate team members wrote in Glenn's yearbook, "Dear 'Unc,' I should know you rather well. I studied, slept, debated and traveled with you, and the highest compliment I can give is to say that you are still as fresh, clear, and witty as the day I first saw you. Good luck in law and politics."

Another commencement speaker wrote this: "Here's to Glen Cogswell, fellow commencement speaker. You've done swell in high school being on the debate squad, vice president of our class, etc. Let's see you keep it up next year..."

Another complimentary note from a friend reads: "Glen, remember English and all the fun. Congratulations on all the debate honors and being speaker. No use wishing you luck with your personality and ability to make friends. You're sure to get it."

His debate partner Harry G., wrote: "...You as a politician and vice-president have been a great success. This isn't my last rebuttal, Glenn, so it's all the truth, you are the best friend I have ever had; you know that's saying an awful lot, when you consider all my friends. But sincerely, I certainly hope to remain a friend of a boy I have always admired. Your selection of girls is the tops – wish I had some courage, and a little of your personality. Receiving distinction in debate was certainly coming to you... *Best of luck, Glenn, to you and all the Cogswells (especially any little ones that may come along) Harry.*"

'He Shines All *Over*'

"To the brilliant lad in History IV, he's so brilliant, he shines all *over.* Billye S."

"Dear Glenn, May you always have the very best of luck and happiness that you so well deserve. I hope you keep on with debating, etc. Your commencement speech was *very* good. (Queen) Pat L."

From a teacher: "I have watched your high school career with interest. I hope you will continue to use your ability in public speaking."

And the principal: "Keep working! You have *it!*"

From Topeka High School to Sunflower Boys' State in Wichita

A class of 575 graduated from Topeka High School on Friday, May 19, 1939.

During the summer of 1939, Glenn went to Wichita with twenty-eight boys, most from Topeka, as the Shawnee County delegation to the Sunflower Boys' State in Wichita where he was elected lieutenant governor. His frequent debate partner, Bill Everett, was elected governor. Boys State, sponsored by the American Legion, is an event that taught promising young men about community leadership and participation in the processes of government.

Governor Payne Ratner, who came to speak at the inauguration ceremony, said, "Honestly, I have never seen such a fine group of clean-cut, intelligent, American youths as I did at the Boys' State. Those lads are a credit to their parents and their communities; and by giving them this training in citizenship, the American Legion is doing a real service to the state and the nation. Those lads are capable of doing great things."

Ratner told the audience, "This month, boys in Kansas and many other states are learning just how government affects their life, liberty and happiness. Such knowledge is essential to the life of a useful citizen.

Lieutenant Governor Glenn Cogswell, 17, assumed his duties as president and presiding officer of the senate. Governor Bill Everett recommended to his general assembly that it pass a measure making compulsory Wasserman tests (a test for venereal disease) for all couples contemplating marriage. The political parties for Boys' State were the Federalists and the Nationalists. Glenn was a Federalist. *The Federalist Courier* stated that, "According to Lt. Gov. Cogswell, the bill for compulsory Wasserman tests will probably not pass the House where the Nationalists have the way, because the Nats will be afraid to take the test."

"Social disease is one of the nation's most costly problems, and Kansas is far behind in efforts to control it," Gov. Everett said.

He also "lambasted the Kansas highway department as 'the most expensive in the country' and told the general assembly it should be taken out of politics and placed under civil service. The third recommendation was that a joint committee system be implemented, for both legislative bodies instead of each having their own, which he considered a waste and 'faulty.'"

Washburn College, 1939-1943

Glenn was elected president of the freshman class of Washburn College in 1939-1940 and played forward for Washburn's basketball team in 1940-1941. In 1941-42 he was selected by a group of officers from Fort Riley as "most decorative." The Fort Riley officers selected the late Royce Palmer as the "most decorative" woman. The two are featured in full-page photos in the 1942 Kaw (Washburn yearbook).

In 1941-1942 Glenn was elected president of Washburn University

Student Council. The previous spring, Washburn's new constitution provided that any individual could run for class office, rather than seek the nomination of his party.

"University politics swing into action this week with the announcement by Glen Cogswell, President of the student council, of plans drawn up by the recently-appointed election committee for carrying out and supervising the election of all class officers next Friday," the university paper announced.

According to Cogswell and the committee, any student may get his name on the ballot for one of the class offices upon submission of an official petition bearing the legal number of names by 1 p.m. next Wednesday. These petitions are available in the library today.

Anyone may carry a petition. The petition must be signed by either 20 percent of the class, in which the individual is seeking office, or by 35 members of the class. This would mean only 11 or 14 signatures are needed on senior or junior petitions.

To make the petition valid, it must bear the signature of the person for whom nomination is being sought.

"This is done to prevent an individual who does not want to take the job from being pushed into something over which he has no control," said Cogswell.

With reference to the new policy regarding non-party affiliation, Glenn was quoted as saying, "I think this will be the most democratic election to be held here for many years. For once any individual may seek office if he cares to."

In 1943, Glenn, along with four other Washburn seniors, was chosen to enter training for a commission as ensign in the navy through officer's training at Northwestern University's Midshipman's School in Chicago and was called into active service as an Ensign, United States Naval Reserve in 1943.

In 1942-1943, Glenn was a member of *Who's Who Among Students in American Universities and Colleges*, was rush captain for the Phi Delta Theta fraternity, executive secretary of the collegiate Young Republicans of the state, and received a call to Sagamore, one of the highest honors of the student body. He graduated in absentia from Washburn University with an A.B. degree in 1943.

Washburn University to Omaha Beach

Glenn frequently wrote home from Europe during the year of the D-Day invasion. Like thousands of other young boys in the 1940s, his goals and plans for his life had to take a back seat to his service to his country. He wrote to his parents:

"Well, we're all hoping and praying that the New Year will bring victory, or if that isn't possible, bring us near to it. At least, it would bring us together for a few days.

"I hope they didn't take Ralph and won't take Carroll for a while, anyway. I've seen too much of both the Army and Navy to want any of my brothers in it – but there's not much anyone can do about it if the war continues. I understand Hitler speaks tonight shortly after midnight. That should be interesting. Those Hienies [Germans] seem bent on fighting to the death.

"Happy New Year –I'll be seeing you. Love, Your son, Glenn"

Final Words

Some final thoughts: Always do your best. Give your life to Jesus and after you have given it to him, live for him every day, because God created you and wants you to "shine all over." I understand how life can come along and erode your values, but I also know how God can both soften the blow of painful events in life and turn them into triumph.

The Christian life can be like swimming upstream because when you identify with Jesus Christ you are going against the grain of this world. But remember this world is corrupt, and following in its ways will only lead to misery in both this life and the next.

If you are already a Christian and can look at your life and tell the story of how Jesus Christ changed your life, you will gain in many ways. You will gain self-knowledge, you will gain knowledge of God and you may be able to help somebody else who is looking for what you have but does not know how to find it.

Don't let the powers of darkness (Ephesians 6:12) pull you down. Jesus Christ, when he died on the cross for our sins, broke their power over whoever will simply turn in faith to God and let go of their own way and yield to God's way. You will not be sorry.

If you choose to take up your cross daily and follow Jesus, you will encounter opposition, but don't give up. As soon as you discover the truth that sets you free you become public enemy number one to the devil. But don't let him steal your song!

Meanwhile, you may contact me at carolyncogswell@yahoo.com.

COGSWELL FAMILY – SOME IMPORTANT DATES

1888, February 23 – Susie Alma Schisler born. Dies March 8, 1888.

1889, February 20 - Carl Clifford Cogswell born in Pretty Prairie, Kansas. His mother was Eliza Jane O'Leary, his father, George Kirkpatrick Cogswell (January 9, 1867 - October 7, 1949). Dies May 7, 1975.

1910, February 23 – Wedding of Carl Clifford Cogswell and Susie Alma Schisler.

1922, February 1 – Glenn Dale Cogswell born on a farm in Pretty Prairie, Kingman County, Kansas, the youngest of four sons to Susie Alma Schisler (1888-1988) and Carl Clifford Cogswell (1889-1975). The four boys are: Carroll Clayton (1912-1994), Kenneth Marvel (1915-1995), Ralph Eldon (1917-2004) and Glenn Dale (1922-2011).

1922 – Carl Clifford Cogswell elected state lecturer of Kansas State Grange, serving as state master from 1928 to 1946.

1933 - Carl Clifford Cogswell, Susie Cogswell and four boys move from farm in Pretty Prairie to Topeka, Kansas.

1938-1939 – Glenn Cogswell in his senior year of high school, an honor student, on the debate team, delivers a speech at graduation.

1939-1940 – Glenn elected president of the freshman class of Washburn College (now Washburn University), Topeka, Kansas.

1940-1941 – Glenn plays forward for Washburn's basketball team.

1941-1942 – Glenn elected president of Washburn University Student Council.

1943 – Glenn graduates in absentia from Washburn University with an A.B. degree.

1943 – Glenn Cogswell enters officer's training at Northwestern Midshipman's School in Chicago and is called into active service as an Ensign, United States Naval Reserve.

1943-1946 – Glenn Cogswell serves as lieutenant in the U.S. Navy Reserve, including D-Day Invasion at Normandy.

1945 - May 1, marriage of Glenn Cogswell and Jean (Jeanette) Hallewell (later Jeanne Cogswell and Jeanne Hagen), in Southampton, England.

1946, February – Jean travels to the U.S. from England.

1946, November 25 – Birth of Carolyn Cogswell in Topeka, Kansas.

1947, January – Mr. and Mrs. (Elsie Amelia Rose Hall) Thomas Luke George Hallewell arrive from Southampton, England.

1947 – Glenn Cogswell receives a J.D. from Washburn law school, Topeka, and admitted to the Kansas Bar.

1949-1951 – Glenn Cogswell serves as Judge of the Court of Topeka, Kansas (elected, 1948).

1949 – September 21 – David Glenn Cogswell born in Topeka, Kansas.

1951-1957 – Glenn Cogswell served as judge of the probate and juvenile courts of Shawnee County (elected in 1950, 1952, and 1954; serves in public office 1948-1957).

1954 – Glenn Cogswell becomes president of the Kansas Probate Judges Association.

1956 - Glenn and Jeanne divorced.

1957 – Glenn marries second wife, Irene. They are married eleven or twelve years.

1958 – Glenn defeated in bid for election as lieutenant governor of Kansas.

1963 - Summer – Carolyn travels to Mexico with twenty-five high school juniors.

1963 – Jean marries Jerry Hagen; they are married eleven years.

1964 – Carolyn graduates from Topeka West High School, Topeka, Kansas.

1965–January 25, Laura Anne Hagen born (Jeanne's daughter with Jerry).

1966 – Tornado in Topeka, Kansas.

1968 – Carolyn graduates from Kansas University with bachelor's degree in secondary education with a major in Spanish and a minor in French.

1968-1969 – Carolyn teaches Spanish just one school year at West Junior High in Kansas City, Kansas, during her first year out of college.

1968 – Glenn married his third wife; they are married for about fifteen years.

1969–July, 15, Michael Keith Hagen is born (Jeanne's son with Jerry).

1975-1976 - Carolyn took art classes at Kansas University while living in Lawrence, Kansas.

1977 – Carolyn's first trip to England with her first husband, (divorced in 1978).

1979 – Carolyn's second trip to England, alone, to see her Auntie Agnes.

1979 – Carolyn moves to Costa Mesa, California, to play country music at motel lounge.

1979, July 15 – attends an evangelical meeting in Anaheim, California, where Hal Lindsay prays for Carolyn who surrenders her life to Christ and experiences salvation (age thirty-three).

1979, July (the next Sunday) – to Calvary Chapel, meets Chuck Smith, stays four months in Costa Mesa at "The Lord's House," a residential facility and ministry for new converts.

1979 – Carolyn returns to Topeka to share her new-found faith in Jesus.

1982-1986 – Carolyn lives and works in Louisiana (where she marries her second husband whom she meets there; this marriage lasts about two and a half years).

1990-1992 – Carolyn attends graduate school at Oklahoma State University in Stillwater, Oklahoma. Her master's thesis is a study comparing children from intact versus divorced families relative to their relationship with their grandparents.

1992 – Glenn Cogswell comes to Stillwater, Oklahoma, to see Carolyn receive her master's degree in family relations and child development with an emphasis in family studies.

1994 – Marriage of Glenn Cogswell to Peggy Anderson to whom he is married eighteen years.

1996 - Carolyn receives her Ph.D. in human ecology with an emphasis in child development at the University of Tennessee in Knoxville in the summer.

1997 - Fall – Carolyn teaches Spanish at McMinn County High School in Athens, Tennessee.

1998 – Spring, through Spring, 2000 – Carolyn teaches at Morehead State University, Morehead, Kentucky.

1999 – Carolyn and David goes to Cogswell Family Association Reunion in Salem, Massachusetts with Glenn and Peggy.

2000 Fall through spring 2005 – Carolyn teaches at Southeast Missouri State University in Cape Girardeau.

2005 - Carolyn takes three journalism courses while a faculty member in Missouri.

2005-2007 – Carolyn works as a reporter for three weekly newspapers.

2005, November - Carolyn moves to Ellington, Missouri, to work as reporter for the *Reynolds County Courier*.

2006, November – Carolyn moves to Osage City, Kansas, to work as staff writer for the *Osage County Herald* (later the *Osage County Herald-Chronicle*).

2007, August – Carolyn moves to Overland Park, Kansas, to work as education reporter for the *Johnson County Sun*. Receives a second place award for best education story from the Kansas Press Association and is later laid off along with the publisher, editor and several reporters.

2008, July – Carolyn moves back to Topeka, begins work as preschool assistant teacher.

2008, February 1 - Glenn's 86th birthday, still living at home.

2009 – Glenn to nursing home in Topeka.

2011, February 7 – Glenn Cogswell passes away, and Peggy the following July.

BIBLIOGRAPHY

Cogswell, Helen Trostel. *Cogswell-Haldeman.* Denver: Big Mountain Press, 1966.

Flynn, Don, *Topeka State Journal,* July 9, 1955.

Hart, Archibald. *Helping Children Survive Divorce.* Nashville: Thomas Nelson, 1997.

Jameson, E. O. *The Cogswells in America (1884).*

Markley, Walter M. *Builders of Topeka 1956.* Topeka: Capper, 1956.

Marquardt, Elizabeth. *Between Two Worlds: The Inner Lives of Children of Divorce* (Crown, 2005).

Marquis, Don. *Archy and Mehitabel.* New York: Doubleday, 1916.

Outler, Albert Cook, translated and ed. *The Confessions of St. Augustine,* Mineola, NY: Dover Publications, Inc., 2002.

Pascal, Blaise. *Pens*ées, New York, NY: The Modern Library, 1941.

Prince, Derek. *God's Remedy for Rejection.* New Kensington, PA: Whitaker House, 2002.

Stanley, Charles. *Success God's Way.* Nashville: Thomas Nelson Publishers, 2000.

The American Heritage Dictionary Second College Edition, Boston: Houghton Mifflin Company, Boston: Houghton Mifflin Company, 1982, 1985.

Townsend, Robert. *Topeka Daily Capital,* August 8, 1954. "Divorce is great growing social problem in Kansas."

Utain, Marsha. A monograph, *Stepping Out of Chaos* (1989).

Wallerstein, Judith. *Surviving the Breakup, 1980.*

Wallerstein, Judith S. and Blakeslee, Sandra. *Second Chances: Men, Women and Children a Decade after Divorce.* New York: Bantam, 1989.

Wallerstein, Judith S., Lewis, Julia M. and Blakeslee, Sandra. *The Unexpected Legacy of Divorce.* New York: Hyperion, 2000.

Ware, Eugene F. *The Rhymes of Ironquill.* New York: G.P. Putnam's Sons, 1939.